To Jean
Best wishes
Malcolm Cooper

RELUCTANT WARRIORS

★

MEMORIES OF NATIONAL SERVICE

1945 TO 1960

RELUCTANT WARRIORS

✯

MEMORIES OF NATIONAL SERVICE

1945 TO 1960

MALCOLM COWPER

First published in Great Britain in 2019 by

Bannister Publications Ltd
118 Saltergate
Chesterfield
Derbyshire S40 1NG

Typeset in Palatino Linotype by Escritor Design, Bournemouth

Printed and bound in the UK by CMP UK Ltd, Poole, Dorset

*In memory of all National Servicemen who lost their lives
in the service of their country.*

Contents

INTRODUCTION

B ETWEEN THE END of the Second World War and 1960, over two million men aged 18 or over were conscripted to serve for two years in the Army, the Navy or the RAF. It was called National Service. They were trained to kill and were liable to be killed, yet Britain was no longer at war. Why, then, were they compelled to sacrifice two years of their lives?

One reason was that the government wanted to ensure that never again would the nation be so unprepared for war as it had been in 1939. Conscription for a relatively short period of service would create a reservoir of trained men who could quickly be called up in the event of an emergency.

However, this was not the only reason. After the war, Britain had huge military commitments. She still had an empire, even though it was starting to disintegrate. Independence movements were active in India, Malaya, and Kenya, and large forces were required to police these countries. Palestine, though not a British colony, was ruled by Britain under a League of Nations mandate, but was riven with bitter conflict between Jews who wanted it as their homeland and Arabs determined to keep them out. British troops had the impossible task of keeping the peace. Egypt, with its vital Suez Canal, had been a protectorate under informal British control since the 1880s, but its people now wanted the British out.

The division of Germany into Soviet controlled East and democratic West meant that it had become the frontier of the Cold War, requiring the presence of large numbers of troops on constant standby in case of a Communist invasion.

When war broke out in Korea, Britain felt it necessary to support the USA by sending troops.

At the same time, the government was committed to demobilising the men who had been called up during the war. There was no hope of creating volunteer forces of sufficient numbers to meet the country's vast commitments. The only solution was universal short term compulsory service.

Britain, unlike her continental neighbours, had always resisted conscription, priding herself on having been able to raise volunteer forces when required. It was not until 1916, when most of the men who had flocked to the recruiting offices at the outbreak of the First World War had been killed on the Western Front, that it had reluctantly to be introduced. It ended with the Armistice in 1918 and was not reintroduced until shortly before the start of the Second World War. Conscription had never previously been used in peacetime.

So in 1945 the machinery for calling up young men on their 18th birthday simply carried on, at first for an unspecified period, later fixed at 18 months, which was raised to two years during the Korean War in 1950, and the term 'National Service' came into the language. The majority, some two thirds, went into the Army, while most of the remainder entered the RAF, only a very small number being taken on by the Royal Navy.

Only those who were medically unfit or in reserved occupations such as farming or mining were exempt, although conscientious objection on religious grounds was allowed. Seven years' service in the Merchant Navy also brought exemption. Those who were undergoing apprenticeships could defer their service until they had qualified, and those who intended to go to college or university could either do their National Service first or defer it until after they had graduated. For everyone else it was a matter of answering the summons or going to prison.

Looking back from a 21st Century perspective, it may seem surprising that there was not more resistance to a system that took away two years of a young man's life, with its consequent effects on his relationships and his career.

In the course of my interviews, two reasons were suggested.

Firstly, they had all lived through the Second World War, a time when individual needs had to be sacrificed for the survival of the nation. Young men were imbued with a strong sense of duty and obedience, conditioned to respect authority, to do what they were told and not ask questions. In a society where young people were far more strictly disciplined than they are today, it seemed perfectly natural to submit to conscription. That is not to say that many did not try to avoid it by feigning spurious ailments, but few got away with it.

Secondly, many had seen their fathers, uncles and older brothers putting on a uniform and going off to war. The fact that there was no longer a war did not remove the necessity of being prepared for one, especially during the tense years after 1945, when Russia, our ally during the war, had become a deadly potential enemy. National Service became a rite of passage, a 'toughening up' period of strict discipline which you entered as a boy and came out as a man. An added bonus was that in the days before mass tourism, overseas postings enabled them to travel to faraway places which few of their contemporaries had ever seen, and although they were there on Her Majesty's Service, there were usually opportunities to visit tourist areas.

However, the downside was that National Servicemen could get killed, and many were, in the Korean War, in Malaya, in Cyprus and in Kenya. Unfortunately, I did not manage to make contact with any men who had served in Malaya or Kenya, and only those who served in Cyprus and Suez actually fired a weapon in anger. This book therefore only offers a partial picture of National Service.

This period of peacetime conscription, from 1945 to 1960, is unique in our history, and deserves to be recorded. So I decided to write this book to try to capture the memories and experiences of the men of this generation, conscious of the fact that time to do so is running out. I was heartened by the response I received from my letters in the local press asking those who wished to share their memories of National Service to contact me, and I carried out some sixty interviews. Most are men local to my home in South Wales, but their experiences were exactly the same as those of men from everywhere else in the UK. I found it fascinating to talk to them and listen to their stories that evoke a period that has now passed into history.

This book is not intended to be a work of historical scholarship. I have, wherever possible, provided background details so as to give these stories a context, but the purpose of the book is no more than to provide an collection of memories of men who lived through a unique experience.

Malcolm Cowper
August 2018

BASIC TRAINING

WHETHER THE NEW recruit found himself in the Army, the Navy or the RAF, his first experience of service life was Basic Training, a process designed to strip him of his individuality and mould him into a unit in which orders were obeyed without question and insubordination severely punished. His civilian clothes were parcelled up and sent home, to be replaced by a uniform which might or might not have fitted him. His carefully cultivated hair style disappeared under the barber's ruthless clippers. He was allocated a number, which he had to learn by heart, and by which he would from now on be addressed (or at least by the last three of the eight digits. All my interviewees could remember their numbers, even after more than 60 years!). His home was a bleak barrack room with ten or more beds down each side and a temperamental stove in the middle, and it had to be kept scrupulously clean and tidy. From dawn till dusk he was screamed and sworn at by NCOs as he marched endlessly round the parade ground in a process known as 'square bashing'. His off duty time was spent polishing his boots and buttons to mirror brilliance, applying blanco (bought out of his meagre wages) on his webbing equipment, or ironing knife-edge creases in his trousers. To young men brought up in gentler environments it was a traumatic experience, and many homesick tears were shed as they tried to sleep in their uncomfortable beds.

This period, which could last between six and sixteen weeks, culminated in a passing out parade, to which families would be invited to witness the transformation of their loved ones from callow youths to upstanding young men, proudly performing their immaculate drill routines in perfect unity. From here they would progress to further training units or regiments, where the regime would be more relaxed, the indoctrination process having been completed.

The next move would be a posting, either home or overseas. Package holidays abroad were still some years in the future, so for these young men it was something of an adventure if they were posted overseas, a chance in their off duty time to experience the life and culture of a foreign country. On the other hand, they faced the possibility of encountering enemies who were out to kill them, and over 300 National Servicemen died while on active service overseas.

Most of my interviewees who had been posted overseas went to Germany, Cyprus, Egypt or Libya. Few actually fired a weapon in anger, apart from those who landed at Suez or fought terrorists in Cyprus. Unfortunately, I did not meet any who had served in Malaya or Kenya, two areas where National Servicemen experienced dire conditions and suffered high casualties.

Richard Tadman, who served in the Royal Armoured Corps from 1951 to 1953, wrote an account of his first days of National Service which captures the feelings and experiences of many young men plucked from their comfortable civilian lives and hurled into the harsh world of the armed forces.

"Like thousands of young men in their teens, I was instructed to attend a medical examination held above a local snooker hall. I was passed as A1, the top category for employment in Her Majesty's forces. Asked which force I would like to serve in, I said "The Navy".

"You can't join the Navy" I was told "unless you're prepared to sign on for five years."

"Having no desire to serve more than the statutory two years, I opted for the Army, and was then asked which branch I preferred. Not keen on the infantry, I suggested a tank regiment. This appeared to be a good answer, and I was enlisted in the Royal Armoured Corps.

"Eventually my call-up papers arrived, with a travel warrant and an instruction to report forthwith to Catterick Camp in Yorkshire. By now I was twenty years old and working on a fruit farm in Kent, in a quiet corner of rural England that had, ten years earlier, been on the flightpath of German bombers heading for London. I had never heard of Catterick, and Yorkshire was just a place on a school map, somewhere up north.

"I eventually arrived in Catterick Camp, together with numerous other fresh faced, suited and booted young men, to be greeted by a smart looking sergeant who said "You 'orrible little men are in the Army now and we are going to make SOLDIERS of you!"

"We were kitted out by the Quartermaster Sergeant, who eyed us up and presented us with our battle dress uniforms, black boots, navy berets and numerous items of webbing equipment. The sergeant we had met earlier informed us that we now held the rank of Trooper in the Royal Armoured Corps. We were told our army number, which we had to memorise, issued with pay books numbers one and two, and given the obligatory short back and sides haircut. We had now lost our civilian identity. We were shown to the huts that were to be our home for the next eight weeks.

"We then started our basic training, the Army's way of making us tough, fearless soldiers (well, sort of!). We undoubtedly learned the hard way what discipline really was, and even the streetwise kids soon lost their city swagger. "Do as you're told and we'll get on fine" was the message that was drummed into us. Training consisted mainly of 'square bashing', which consisted of marching and drilling with .303 rifles from the First World War. As a big treat we were shown the Comet tank we would be training on.

"During training our lives would be dominated by a Lance Corporal whom we suspected as having been dropped on his head at birth, which explained his warped sense of humour. An example of this was when he told us we had been "naughty 'orrible little men" and we were to parade in our off-duty time outside our hut with our eating irons (knife, fork and spoon). As we had just had our tea, this seemed a strange request, and we wondered if we were going to a party. However, we soon found out when we were told to get down on our hands and

knees and cut the grass outside the hut, using our knives as shears! We hacked away until we had satisfied the lance corporal, who told us not to be naughty again. We never did find out what naughty thing we had done to deserve this bizarre punishment."

Richard's subsequent service in Germany is described later in the book.

OVERSEAS POSTINGS - GERMANY

IN 1945, FOLLOWING Germany's unconditional surrender, the country was divided into four zones of military occupation, each zone to be controlled by one of the Allied powers: Britain in the north west, France in the south west, the USA in the south and Russia (or the Soviet Union, as it was then called) in the east. The plan was that the occupation of these zones was to continue until de-Nazification had been completed and the country was ready to return to civilian government.

Berlin lay 110 miles inside the Soviet zone, but as the capital city it was itself divided into the same four zones. This was to ensure co-operation between the four powers in the government of the country.

However, the spirit of unity between the Western Allies and the Soviet Union that had existed during the war rapidly evaporated. Josef Stalin, the Soviet dictator, had no intention of returning Germany to free democratic government. Instead, he wanted to add it to the list of East European countries onto which he had forced unelected communist governments which he could control. In 1948 he tried to force the Western Allies out of Berlin by closing the road and rail links to the city. The allies responded by flying in literally everything that was necessary to support the population of two million in the three western sectors, and for eleven months American and British aircraft flew round the clock in and out of Berlin's airports, until finally Stalin realised that the Allies were not going to back down, and lifted the blockade. This became known as the Berlin Airlift, or 'Luftbrucke', as the grateful Germans called it.

It was clear that a unified Germany was now an impossibility, so in 1949 the Western Allies established the Federal Republic of Germany, or West Germany as it was commonly known. In response, the Soviet

Zone became the so-called German Democratic Republic, or East Germany. In Berlin, the allied sector became West Berlin, while East Berlin became the capital of the GDR. Bonn was chosen as the capital of the Federal Republic.

Germany was now the front line between two hostile ideologies: the democratic capitalist West headed by the USA, and the communist East with puppet governments controlled by Moscow. A barbed wire border divided the two blocs, often referred to as the Iron Curtain, and travel between them was severely restricted. This period became known as the Cold War, and lasted for forty years, until the collapse of the Soviet Union in 1989.

Because of the constant threat of an invasion of West Germany by the Soviet Union, a huge military presence was established in the country. The North Atlantic Treaty Organisation (NATO) was set up to guarantee mutual assistance to any of its members in the event of an attack. Britain's contribution to the defence of Germany was the British Army of the Rhine, to which many National Servicemen were posted.

Keith Price

RAF 1947-49

Keith had almost completed his National Service as an RAF radio technician when he was suddenly and unexpectedly posted to Berlin. Here he witnessed the final stages of one of the most remarkable events of the early Cold War years: the Berlin Airlift.

Keith was based at RAF Gatow, where he witnessed the incredible armada of aircraft landing and taking off round the clock, and was impressed by the speed at which the Germans were unloading each aircraft as soon as it had landed. The planes did not always return empty; despite the heavy bombing of the city, some manufacturing still continued, and the aircraft were shipping out the finished goods. However, shortly after his arrival, the road and rail links were reopened, although supplies continued to be brought in by air for some months

Berliners watching a C-54 land at Berlin Tempelhof Airport, 1948;
(United States Air Force Historical Research Agency via Cees Steijger (1991)

in case the communists decided to reinstate the blockade.

Keith, from Abertillery, had always been interested in aircraft. His membership during his youth of the Air Training Corps made the RAF an obvious choice for National Service when he was called up in 1947. He reported first to Padgate, where he was kitted out, and then to West Kirby for basic training. Although the discipline in the RAF was less strict than in the army, new recruits still had to endure a period of 'bull'. Keith recalls the day of arrival when the door of the barrack room was flung open and a sergeant drill instructor stormed in. His face purple with rage, he ordered them off the bunks on which they were relaxing. "Stand by your beds!" he screamed, and proceeded to tell them exactly what he thought of them. This set the pattern for the next twelve weeks.

Keith should then have moved on to Trade School, but the severe winter of 1947 had set back the programme by several weeks. He was sent to Upper Heyford for radio training, but the classes were full, so for much of the time he was just hanging around. He would watch trainee parachutists jumping from the basket of a tethered balloon, and one occasion he accepted the offer to go up in the basket, though not to jump. He found it terrifying, and wondered how anyone could actually find the courage to jump out! At least the barracks there were comfortable and the food was good. Then he was posted to Fairford, in Gloucestershire, where Halifax bombers practised towing troop-carrying gliders. On one occasion he actually flew in a glider, and admired the courage of the paratroopers who, a few years earlier, had gone to war in these fragile, vulnerable craft.

Finally, in December 1947, Keith began a twelve week course as a radio technician at RAF Cranwell, in Lincolnshire, which he recalls as being a very cold place. Postings followed to Chivenor, in Devon, and a rocket range in Bridgwater Bay. Then came the posting to Berlin, which prolonged his service by three months. During his stay he saw little of the ruined city. The presence of unfriendly, glowering Russian soldiers deterred him from straying too far from the airport. After three months he returned to the UK, was discharged, and resumed his job in Barclay's Bank.

Keith enjoyed his National Service, and recalls having a lot of fun, but he never considered staying on. Despite the more relaxed discipline of the RAF, punishment could be severe for serious offences. On one occasion he and a colleague were ordered to escort a miscreant to the military prison at Colchester, a formidable place where the most recalcitrant 'hard cases' were sent (see David Collins's story). He did not resent having to do National Service; it was just something one had to do in those days, like going to school.

Richard Dobbs

Royal Engineers 1958-60

Richard was another National Serviceman who was posted to Berlin, after completing his training as a driver at Aldershot, where he gained a UK civilian driving licence endorsed for military vehicles. He already held a provisional licence, so driving was a fairly obvious choice of trade for him. He had deferred his National Service till he was twenty so as to complete his apprenticeship as a carpenter.

Berlin at that time had not been divided by the Wall. There was a psychological rather than a physical barrier between East and West, and British soldiers were able to go into East Berlin on a military coach once a month, but they had to be in uniform. Richard noticed the glaring contrast between the two halves of the city. West Berlin was by then a thriving, bustling, place, largely rebuilt after the devastation of wartime bombing, whereas East Berlin looked smart enough along the main streets, but this was only a facade, behind which still lay much war damage. Five thousand people a week, no longer willing to tolerate life in a police state, were crossing into West Berlin and heading for freedom and a better standard of living. The country was losing its engineers, its doctors, its teachers, until finally, to stop this haemorrhage of its key workers, the infamous Wall was erected in August 1961, on the ludicrous pretext that it was needed to keep spies out!

In West Berlin there was still some rubble from the war to be cleared, and this was one of the Royal Engineers' jobs. On one occasion an unexploded bomb was discovered, and Richard had to drive the vehicle that was sent to carry out the hazardous task of removing it. The DKW jeep and trailer, bearing flags and 'Danger UXB' signs, pulled up alongside, the bomb was gingerly lifted onto the trailer, which then bounced along the cobbled streets until it reached an area where it could be safely detonated. Thankfully, it did not go off on the precarious journey!

A far safer and more pleasant job for Richard was to be driver for the 'postman'. The Royal Engineers operated the postal service for the Army, and its headquarters were in the stadium where the Nazi

The Olympiastadion in 1936 (Bundesarchiv, Bild 183-R82532 / CC-BY-SA 3.0)

Olympic Games had been held in 1936. The job was something of a 'skive', as not only was Richard excused attendance at parades, but also, as the delivery of the mail was done by lunchtime, the rest of the day could be spent 'hiding' in Toc H (a soldiers' rest and recreation centre founded in the First World War).

Richard found the Berliners friendly and hospitable. They welcomed the presence of British troops, as it provided a safeguard against any possible communist attempt to take over the city, and more civilians were employed by the military than soldiers. Anyone unable to get home for Christmas would be welcomed into German homes, and in fact Richard and one of his pals was the recipient of local hospitality one year. He recalls hearing horror stories from his hosts of the Russian troops who occupied the city at the end of the war, primitive, illiterate men who had never seen a staircase and who washed in toilets.

Within the boundary of West Berlin were large areas of lakes and forests such as the Grunewald and the Havel See. These areas were much appreciated by its citizens, trapped as they were deep inside East Germany, enabling them to escape into the countryside at weekends. Richard spent quite a lot of time at the lakes, not so much for recreation as to practise water crossings and building jetties. As Havel was a working lake, this had to be done at night. An annual map-reading scheme was held, its aim to reach a fixed point in the Grunewald and then have a good 'booze up' afterwards! To make life easier (and somewhat to undermine the object of the exercise) the Irish sergeant in charge would light a fire which anyone who was lost could head for!

Once a year they left the city and travelled into West Germany, to the Pied Piper town of Hamelin. Here, working at night, they once built a bridge across the Haml and took it down again before the river traffic started the next morning.

Next to the camp where Richard was based stood Spandau Prison, where Rudolf Hess, Hitler's deranged former deputy, who in 1941 had flown to Britain on his own initiative to try to seek peace, was now living out his long and lonely imprisonment. He was guarded in turn by troops of the four Allied Powers, Britain, France, the USA and the Soviet Union. The Russians did not want their squaddies to see westerners so only used junior officers for guard duties.

As National Service was coming to an end, the military authorities were anxious to retain manpower levels, and as an encouragement to remain in the Army they raised the pay level to that of regulars, but much as he had enjoyed Berlin, Richard never thought to stay on. His civilian job was kept open for him, of course, but he had lost the opportunity to apply for a trainee manager's job, which left him feeling rather bitter. Nevertheless, he had found National Service very beneficial, in increasing his self-confidence. As he himself said, before he went in he would not even have dared to answer the phone!

George Jeffery

RAF 1955-57

For most of his National Service, George had a comfortable posting in Germany. His work as a signals operator maintaining communication with thirteen other RAF stations (and one Russian!) left him with plenty of time at weekends to go travelling round Germany and Switzerland, often hiking in the mountains. He ran a scout troop which included the Commanding Officer's son, thus ensuring that he was amply provided with camping equipment and other necessaries, including, on one occasion, a delivery of water by tanker. A large house on an estate belonging to the Miele company was also available for his scouts to use. He lived in superb quarters, with German civilians on hand to do his domestic chores. On the base he played hockey and table tennis. When he got leave a flight back to the UK could be arranged. It was easy to forget that his purpose in being in Germany was to be trained to fight a war.

This easy life came to an abrupt but temporary end with the Suez crisis in November 1956. In the build up to the invasion, George suddenly and unexpectedly found himself being hastily trained as a radio operator on a bomber! The situation looked extremely serious, and the possibility of being engaged in a real war became highly likely. Fortunately, the crisis was short lived, and George never got to Egypt, and was able to resume his peaceful life in Germany.

George was born in Battersea, London, on 12th May 1937, which just happened to be the day of King George VI's Coronation. In commemoration of this, his mother received a pram and £5 (more than a week's wages in those days) from the borough council! When war broke out, the family was not evacuated, and George has a hazy memory of the Blitz. He does, however, remember the V1 'doodle bugs' and playing on bomb sites. His National Service began in November 1955 with a week of kitting out at RAF Cardington, in Bedfordshire, followed by basic training at West Kirby. It was a bitterly cold winter, but there was little warmth in the barrack rooms because the stoves remained unlit so that they would not have to be cleaned out the next day! Then came seventeen weeks of signals training at Compton Bassett, where the 'bull' and misery of West Kirby was replaced by a more relaxed regime, with parades only once a month rather than every day. Finally, he was posted to Gutersloh, in Germany, where he spent the rest of his service.

George made several trips to Berlin. The journey across 110 miles of hostile territory was not without its frustrations. Travel could only be at night, with all lights out, and trains were liable to be stopped at any time by border guards for no other reason than to make life inconvenient. There were even rumours of people disappearing en route. Nevertheless, British service personnel were encouraged to make the trip, in order to show the East Germans that they had a right to be there, and to give reassurance to the citizens of West Berlin of their continued protection.

George was very glad, in retrospect, that he did not take up what appeared at the time to be a tempting posting to Christmas Island, where testing of the atomic bomb was taking place. With minimal protection from radiation, volunteers who went there later began to suffer serious illnesses caused by radioactive exposure.

George's National Service brought him close to involvement in a real war in Egypt, which fortunately ended almost before it had begun, and to the reality of the Cold War in Berlin. Apart from that, it was an enjoyable experience which brought him into contact with men from many walks of life and to places where he would otherwise not have gone.

Anthony Jones

RAF Regiment 1953-57

"A bit of a holiday at the Government's expense" was how Anthony described his National Service. 18 years old, with no ties, he decided that he was going to enjoy it and willingly signed on for an extra two years when invited to, which earned him an extra £2 a week on top of the niggardly National Serviceman's pay. Ater basic training he was posted to the RAF Regiment and was sent to RAF Catterick, (next door to the huge Army base) where a drill squad for the Royal Tournament was being trained. This squad had to perform a sequence of drill manoeuvres without a word of command being given, and this became a showpiece of the RAF Regiment for many years. They trained every day for six months under the command of Warrant Officer Danny

Goole, whom Anthony described as "a man you would go to war with, reliable, always on your side."

After the Royal Tournament, Anthony should have been posted to Egypt in the build-up to the Suez invasion, but he unwittingly escaped this posting by overstaying his weekend leave in order to play rugby. While at his home in Sarn, near Bridgend, he was asked to play for Maesteg, but if he did so he would not be back at Catterick by midnight, and would face a spell on 'jankers' .So an obliging local GP gave him a sick note

Anthony Jones, studio portrait

to explain his overdue return. When he got back he discovered that the rest of his unit had been deployed to Suez, but he was too late. Instead, he was posted to Germany.

RAF Wahn was both a military base and a civilian airport serving Bonn and Cologne. The primary function of the RAF Regiment was the defence of airfields, and Anthony's squadron deployed around the perimeter and practiced using Bofors guns. He was now a gunnery instructor. There was not a lot to do apart from training, but a diversion to their rather uneventful life came with a NATO exercise at Kiel, on the Baltic, where they practised firing at drogues towed by aircraft.

At least there was plenty of sport available, which suited Anthony fine. He played rugby for the base and also boxed. He took full advantage of the privileges accorded in the forces for those who were good at sport, such as being excused guard duties so that they could train.

The Warrant Officer who organised the boxing was very keen for Anthony to become more involved, but he refused to do so, preferring to concentrate on rugby. This did not please the WO, and shortly afterwards Anthony found himself posted to RAF Wunsdorf, near Hannover. Whether the WO had engineered this out of spite he never found out, but it illustrated the power of senior NCOs and the need to keep on the right side of them.

The station Commanding Officer at Wahn was an ex-rugby player, and he organised travel all over Germany for the team to play other bases. One trip was to Berlin, and while they were there they decided to see something of this bizarrely divided city. As they drove along Stalinallee, the long main street through the east zone, they noticed that what appeared to be solid buildings were, in fact, facades, behind which were still the remains of wartime bombing, whereas in the west much of the war damage had been cleared up. At that time there was no Wall and it was easy to travel on the metro (S Bahn) from one zone to another. However, on one occasion they inadvertently got off in the Soviet zone and went into a bar. Immediately all conversation stopped, for although they were in 'civvies' their dress was recognisably western. They hastily left and caught the next train back to the British Zone!

They were also able to visit the former Nazi concentration camp at Belsen, though there was very little to see other than large mounds of earth, and Anthony was surprised that it had become a tourist attraction so soon after the war.

Another time a rugby trip to Paris was organised. This was to play a French Air Force team at Fontainbleu, but it was also the weekend of the Wales v France game, which they were able to go and watch. Afterwards they were given free time in Paris and as they were not expected back in barracks till the next morning it can be assumed that they had a good time!

All servicemen received a cigarette ration, something which would be unacceptable these days. Anthony did not smoke, and sold his ration to an entrepreneur who sold them on the black market in Hannover.

Anthony generally found the German civilians friendly, but at Wunstorf he encountered verbal hostility from some German youths while he was guard commander. He told his men to ignore them, and not rise to the bait, pointing out that these youths may have been resentful at having lost fathers and older brothers in the war, or simply through having lost the war.

Having signed on for the extra years, and therefore being a regular,

Anthony was entitled to preparation for civilian life as he came to the end of his service. Though a toolmaker by trade, he had decided to join the police force, and was sent to Hamburg for three days to shadow the police there and learn a little of what the job involved. He was taken on a tour of the city, which included the notorious 'Reeperbahn' in the city's red light district, where some three years later a gang of four scruffy teenage musicians known as the Beatles would cut their teeth in its seedy night clubs.

He did, in fact, join the Glamorgan Police, but after several years he left and went back to his former trade as a toolmaker, in order to earn better wages.

Harry Lowman

Royal Army Education Corps 1957-59

Attitudes towards National Service varied enormously. Some men spent the entire two years resenting every moment and crossing off the days until the longed-for 'demob'; others took the view that this was a once-in-a-lifetime opportunity for new experiences and were determined to make the most of it. In the latter category was Harry Lowman, who during his service not only took advantage of his access to theatres and opera houses in Germany and Italy but also learned to speak German. He also enjoyed a great social life, with both British and German friends.

After leaving Newbury Grammar School in 1955, Harry deferred his National Service to study Classics at Edinburgh University, but, in his own words, 'failed miserably'. This left him no choice but to await call up, which duly came. To his disappointment he was rejected by the Navy and the RAF because of his eyesight, but was deemed A1 for the Army.

His basic training, which began in March 1957, took place with the Royal Hampshire Regiment in Winchester. "We de-pimpled our boots" he recalls "with the heated back of a spoon handle, till, eventually flattened, they would glow under layers of spit and polish. We pressed uniforms to perfection, were taught to march in an orderly fashion, cleaned latrines, were harassed by sergeants and given lectures on sexual health, including an intimate American Forces film in glorious technicolour about venereal diseases, which had even the hardiest recruits passing out in droves. I learned how to scream as I dismembered the enemy with my bayonet (only we didn't have bayonets), fired a rifle with remarkable accuracy (or in my case luck), and was forced to sing as we marched to the rifle range on the outskirts of the city. 'Singing the Blues', a popular ditty at the time, kept us all in perfect step with one another."

Because of his education, Harry was earmarked for officer training, which he "politely refused and opted instead for the Royal Army Education Corps". This meant a move to the Army School of Education at Beaconsfield, where he trained for three months to be a teacher. As such, he was automatically promoted to the rank of sergeant "so that we could at least have some authority over our future charges". He also enjoyed the corresponding increase in pay.

The RAEC, which began life in 1846 as the Corps of Army Schoolmasters, was set up to meet the educational needs of the non-commissioned ranks, and to properly equip soldiers for civilian life. Harry taught mainly maths and English, but he also taught "a soupçon of history and geography as required".

When the time came for choosing a posting, Harry opted for Hong Kong, never expecting, in those days before cheap air flights to anywhere in the world, that he would ever travel there under his own steam. To his disappointment, he did not get Hong Kong, but was instead posted to Germany, which was at least overseas.

His posting was to Hildesheim, one of the oldest cities in Germany. Like Dresden, it had been heavily bombed early in 1945, despite being of little military significance. Its centre, once rich with Mediaeval half-timbered buildings, was flattened, its historic cathedral and other churches reduced to rubble. However, by the time Harry arrived, twelve years later, many of these ancient buildings were being lovingly restored or rebuilt.

On March 22, 1945, Hildesheim was the key target of the Allied Bomber Command. Almost 74% of the buildings in the town were destroyed or damaged during the attack, including nearly the entire historical city centre.

One of Harry's duties was to assist in running the 'public' library at the Education centre, which was open to all ranks and their wives, but his memories of his work as a teacher are hazy; much more vividly remembered is what he did with the rest of his time. "I was in Germany, and I would learn the language while I had this God-given opportunity, and I would make the most of my time there. I was certainly not going to spend my time, as many of the squaddies did, in my pit reading racy Hank Janson novels."

There was no shortage of places to socialise in the town, including cafes "offering temptations the like of which we had never seen before", and in his off-duty hours he would go with a group of colleagues for 'Kaffee und Kuchen', Schnitzel with remoulade sauce or a 'Bauernfruh-stuck' (farmer's breakfast). To establish social contact with the local people, he and Greg, a colleague, approached the authorities to set up an Anglo-German club, and having been given permission, obtained and decorated a hall in the education centre. "A bit of publicity around town and willing volunteers made certain that our first meeting was a tremendous success, with a goodly number of young Germans and British conscripts and a total lack of enmity." Most memorable was the Christmas party, where "hundreds of candles shed such a magical light on the proceedings that for the first time in my life it really felt like Christmas." These could have caused a major conflagration, but it all passed off peacefully without incident.

The German winter offered great opportunities for fun in the snow. A trip by the club to the Hartz Mountains gave Harry his first taste of ski-ing. However, it was something of a disaster, as one of his skis became detached and ended up getting smashed. Much more successful, however, was sledging on the Galgenberg (Gallows

Hildesheim after the bombing raid on 22 March 1945.

Hill) near the camp, whose 164 metre slope provided exhilarating, if somewhat dangerous, runs.

Harry had plenty of opportunity to indulge his love of music. He often went to the Stadttheater (Municipal Theatre) in Hildesheim, which staged operas and operettas as well as plays, and to performances elsewhere in the town, such as Bach's Christmas Oratorio in the magnificent St Michaelkirche. A short train journey away was the rebuilt Hanover Opera House, where he took his parents and sister, as well as some German friends, to see 'Madame Butterfly'. On a camping trip to Italy he and a friend went to an open air opera in the magnificent Baths of Caracalla in Rome, where "we watched the best performance of 'Aida' ever, supping red wine under a warm Italian sky, without a care in the world!" Nor were his musical experiences confined to classical; he once attended a jazz concert given by the great Louis Armstrong, and, even more significantly, met him afterwards, though he cannot now recall where that was.

Harry took every opportunity to practice his German, and as he became more proficient he decided to put himself in for a GCE O Level in the language. He was duly sent to sit the exam at the Bergen-Hohne Garrison on Luneberg Heath, and as he could not return to Hildesheim until the next day he decided to visit the former Bergen Belsen concentration camp, where some 50,000 inmates had died, including Anne Frank and her sister Margaret. Most of it had been razed to the ground with flame throwers following an outbreak of typhus, but the vast mounds of earth marking mass graves gave grim testimony to the atrocities that had been committed in that place.

Harry led a full and eventful social life, with parties, barbecues, dancing and drinking (not always in moderation!) with both British and German friends, some of whom have remained in contact to this day. His military duties were so few and far between that he could almost forget he was a soldier. "Little more than a teacher in khaki uniform, I never went on parade, never fired a rifle again, never went on exercise, never saw action... I led a very cushy existence."

There was one occasion, however, when he was obliged to go on a fairly leisurely route march, during which the Warrant Officer, leading it from behind, commented "You've a fine pair of child-bearing hips, Sergeant Lowman!" This became the title of a memoir which Harry wrote many years later, which he kindly made available to me, and from which I have extensively quoted.

Harry's last night in Germany, on 21st February 1958, was celebrated with "a pub crawl round Hildesheim during which I got hopelessly drunk". He returned to the UK with a massive hangover and a glowing report from his CO, Major Griffin.

He was finally demobilised on 24th March, but remained nervously in the reserves until September 1962. "These three years in the Army Emergency Reserve were a period of great uncertainty for me, as the Cold War was in full swing, the Berlin Wall was erected, Russia exploded the hydrogen bomb and the Cuban missile crisis took place, and I dreaded being recalled to service." To his great relief, he never was.

After leaving the army, Harry did a variety of jobs, but was eventually persuaded by a friend to become a teacher, and at the age of 29 he started a London External degree course at Manchester College of Commerce followed by a postgraduate teacher training course at Southampton University.

Summing up, Harry said "National Service had been for me a truly wonderful experience and without doubt the best two years of my life."

Russell Jones

Royal Engineers 1955-57

Russell was 24 and married when he began his National Service. He had obtained deferment while he completed his student apprenticeship in electrical engineering. When he was called up, he opted for the Royal Engineers, and did his basic training at Aldershot. He was then posted to 26 Field Engineer Regiment in Germany, based in the town of Hamelin, of Pied Piper fame, where the troops were housed in former SS barracks. Never having been abroad before, and expecting everything to be totally different, he was disappointed to see, in the window of a local shop, a display of boxes of Persil!

Russell was assigned to the regiment's training unit, whose commanding officer, Captain Chollerton, was far more interested in flying his glider than carrying out his military duties. He appointed Russell his training clerk and left him to get on with it, so for the rest of his time in Germany he organised the training for the regiment. In recognition of his responsibilities he was promoted to corporal.

When he had married the previous year, he knew that he and his wife, Joy, would be separated for a long time if he was posted overseas. Happily, however, a solution was found, when Russell was asked if he would like to bring his wife over to do 'house guarding' with him. Many of the properties in the town had been requisitioned for army personnel, and there was often a gap of several weeks between one family leaving and another moving in. While they stood empty they were liable to be vandalised, so a couple of 'squaddies' would occupy them as house guardians while they stood empty. If Joy was prepared to put up with frequent house moves, she could come over, and they could be together. Naturally, she took little persuading, and within a few weeks the couple were happily reunited.

For the next nine months they lived a cuckoo-like existence, briefly occupying one house after another, moving nine times in all. They had to put up with constantly packing and unpacking, and of going through the military ritual of 'marching out', where every item down to the last teaspoon had to be checked and accounted for. Eventually they were given permanent quarters and could lead a more settled life.

To occupy her time during the day, Joy set up a kindergarten for service children, a facility which was much appreciated by the mothers, who were then free to go shopping or meet friends. In the evenings and

Russell Jones, studio portrait

at weekends, she and Russell enjoyed the social life of the base or went on excursions around Germany. One of these was to the Möhne Dam, the target of the famous wartime RAF raid immortalised in the film 'The Dam Busters'. On one occasion Russell had the opportunity to watch Manchester United play, little realising that in just a few months' time the team would be decimated by the terrible air crash in Munich.

However, they could never lose sight of the fact that a vast hostile army lay just a few kilometres away. On the other

Russell Jones on exercise on Sennelager Heath

side of the border dividing East and West Germany were the forces of the Warsaw Pact, the communist countries controlled by Moscow. This was the period of the Cold War, and ever present was the nightmare possibility of a nuclear strike, but if conventional land forces were used, NATO had to be ready. To prepare for this, the regiment went on month-long exercises on Sennelager Heath, where battlefield conditions were simulated. The troops had to live under canvas, or even sleep under their vehicles or in foxholes, stand guard twenty four hours a day and be roused from their slit trenches in the middle of the night.

Preparations were also in place for the hasty evacuation of civilians in the event of an attack. All families had to have a 'flap box' containing essential items. If the order came to leave, only these boxes could be taken. Everything else would have to be left. Fortunately , none of these measures had to be carried out, and the collapse of the Soviet Union in 1989 consigned the Cold War to history.

Reflecting on his National Service Russell felt that overall it had been a positive and beneficial experience. He had not welcomed being called up so soon after his marriage, but having his wife with him for most of his posting to Germany made it an enjoyable time for both of them.

John Cuttriss

RAF 1959-62

John was among the last to be called up for National Service, and he almost managed to miss it altogether. After leaving school he served an apprenticeship as a painter and decorator, and delayed his final exams for a year, but by September 1959 he could put it off no longer. Just six months later, National Service ended.

On the advice of his brother, he opted for the RAF, but he had to make a decision. He could serve the compulsory two years, do an optional third year, or, with his qualifications, he could sign on for nine years as a doper. (This title had nothing to do with drugs! It was an archaic term left over from the First World War, when aeroplanes were coated with dope to strengthen their fabric skins. By John's time a doper sprayed the metal skins of aircraft and applied their markings and numbers.) This would mean automatic promotion to corporal, with all the privileges that that entailed, but John's fiancee was not at all happy with the idea of becoming a service wife, so he decided to sign on for three years as a teleprinter operator instead. This would considerably boost his weekly wage from one pound eight shillings (£1.40) to three pounds ten shillings (£3.50). Other benefits included a better quality uniform, extra leave and the higher status of a regular rather than a National Serviceman, who tended to be regarded as the lowest form of service life!

However, it would be some time before he got near a teleprinter. First there was ten weeks 'square bashing' at RAF Bridgnorth. Interspersed with drill were lectures on a variety of topics, including sexual health, and they were warned, when off duty in town, to avoid the 'Wolverhampton Wanderers'. These were not local football supporters but predatory females who might leave the unwary airman with a medical condition he had not been expecting! Once a week there was 'bull night', when every square inch of the hut had to be polished ready for inspection. The incentive was the radio. There was just one between four huts, and the smartest had the radio for a week.

John's hut was the best of the four drill units, and received an unexpected reward by being chosen to line the route along Horseguards Parade for the visit in 1960 of President de Gaulle of France. Unfortunately this meant missing their passing out parade but it was worth it for the honour of being involved in such an important state occasion.

Basic training over, John was posted to No 3 Radio School at RAF Compton Bassett. Their days were no longer spent square bashing, but learning to touch type and get acquainted with the teleprinter, which was cutting edge communications technology in this pre-computer age. Twelve weeks later he was moved again, this time to RAF Scampton, home of the wartime 617 'Dam Busters' Squadron. Here they practised QRA (Quick Reaction Alert), where the Vulcan bombers had to be ready to take off at four minutes' notice in response to the threat of a Russian nuclear attack. John's role in this was to receive, process and deliver signal instructions to pilots waiting in readiness.

Soon afterwards John was on the move again, this time to Pitreavie Castle in Scotland, a 17th Century manor house acquired by the Ministry of Defence in 1938 and was a joint Navy and RAF station. It was from here that the Battle of the Atlantic and the hunt for the Tirpitz had been planned during the war, and it was now playing an important role in the Cold War as a communications centre. Here John became acquainted with the curious Naval tradition of treating every shore establishment as though it were a ship, with its own 'HMS' title. Leaving the camp was 'going ashore', and catching a bus was 'catching a liberty boat'. Once John was reprimanded by a Naval officer for not 'saluting the quarter deck', which was a flag atop a pile of stones!

John was now a long way from his home town of Chesterfield, Derbyshire, but he discovered that it was possible to exchange postings with someone who also wanted to be closer to home, and he found a lad called Jock McKenzie, from Perth, who had been posted to the North Regional Air Traffic Control Centre at Barton Hall, near Preston. A swap was arranged, and a few weeks later John was heading south to Preston while Jock took his place at Pitreavie.

It was now much less of a journey home, although it usually involved hitch hiking to avoid an expensive train fare. In those days anyone in uniform could easily get a lift, and if fact John got a regular ride with the driver of a sugar beet lorry that did weekly deliveries between Preston and Chesterfield.

John's job at Barton Hall involved plotting the military and civilian aircraft along the various corridors, and although the regime was relaxed, the attitude was totally professional. He was there from September 1960 to April 1961, when he received notification of his next posting, this time overseas. He was to go to RAF Rheindahlen, in Germany.

Rheindahlen was the communications centre for all NATO forces. It was the size of a small town, and had shops, cafes, bars, a swimming pool and a cinema. In contrast to the Spartan huts in which he had once lived, he and four others now shared a centrally heated room with showers and laundry facilities. The work involved sending and receiving teleprinter messages. most of which were of mundane routine matters. However, things hotted up in August 1961 when the Berlin Wall went up, and suddenly the prospect of a Third World War briefly loomed up. Sometimes the communications centre was dispersed and set up in an undisclosed destination, so as to be prepared for a possible war situation. During this time they lived under canvas.

John and his mates took advantage of off-duty time to travel, visiting, among other places, Dusseldorf, Amsterdam and Königswinter, where they visited the famous 'Drachenfels' (Dragon's Rock), the ruined castle that overlooks the Rhine. Life in Rheindahlen was pleasant, but home and family still seemed a long way away, and letters from home were always eagerly received. Finally came demob, but even then he still remained on the reserve for the next two years. During this time he received one shilling and sixpence (7.5p) a day. In 1964 he had to attend a two-week refresher course in Plymouth, and only after that was his National Service finally over.

Although John had tried to avoid National Service, he had found it enjoyable and beneficial. He did not regret his decision to sign on for three years. He may have lost out on civilian earnings but the extra year had given him a much broader range of experience.

Peter Millis

RAF 1957-59

Peter was not looking forward to National Service. He had heard frightening (and no doubt exaggerated) stories from those who had been through it. It was an unwanted interruption to his studies, and it meant putting his marriage plans on hold. In order to complete his architectural studies he had been granted deferment, but having reached 25 he could put it off no longer, despite still having a thesis to complete.

He opted for the RAF, where he had hoped to be a fighter plotter, but this role was becoming obsolete. They were now called Air Defence Operators, working at electronic screens, tracking and reporting on aircraft movements, and keeping a watchful eye out especially for Soviet intruders. After 'square bashing' at West Kirby (including camping in the hills of North Wales) and trade training at Middle Wallop, Peter was posted to RAF Jever, in Germany. He describes the accommodation

Group in No 1 Dress. Peter Mills in back row left, with moustache

there as dismal and the 24 hour shift working arrangements dreary, although the surrounding countryside and the small town of Jever were delightful. The radar station in which he worked was several miles away, and he was bussed there and back each day. During this time he went on a Cold War exercise in which he had to spend three or four days entombed underground!

When he arrived at Jever, he spent the first few weeks on duty repainting the radar display table. This was because his superiors had found out he had "something to do with drawings" because he was a student of architecture! Expecting to be in Germany for the next 18 months, he planned to wait until the summer before exploring the country , and was dismayed to be suddenly told he was one of three people who had to be transferred back to 'Blighty' to fill unexpected vacancies.

However, this turned out to be to his advantage. He was posted to RAF Wartling, a Ground Control Interception station in East Sussex, where the atmosphere was more relaxed then in Jever and he was able to continue with his unfinished thesis. He was doing the same job but with more up-to-date equipment. The protected underground operations room was entered via an innocuous looking farmhouse, only the mass of aerials surrounding the site giving any indication that it was not what it pretended to be.

The radar station was located overlooking Pevensey Marshes and near Herstmonceux, with the domestic camp a few miles away on the outskirts of Bexhill and only a mile from the local beach. Fighter Command hours were Monday to Friday with alternate days of mornings and afternoons (and evenings if there was night flying), so there was plenty of flexible time off, and every other weekend was a long one from lunchtime Friday to Monday afternoon. As well as travelling home to South Wales, from Worthing Peter was able to visit an aunt who lived in Surrey, and to meet up with other friends from camp whose homes were nearby. Sometimes equipment needed servicing and 'stand down' meant finding something else for the men to do. On one occasion this involved a visit to a brewery in Eastbourne - with samples!

Peter Mills on 'Demob Day'

Once during trade training, Peter and others were lined up to fly in a jet fighter, but the weather became unsuitable and it was cancelled. Many RAF National Servicemen were given the opportunity to go up in an aircraft, and most took advantage of this unique experience.

Despite his initial fears, Peter said that National Service had been good for him, broadening his mind after a life spent up till then mainly in studying. He made some good friends, one of whom he has kept in touch with ever since. The job at Worthing had been interesting, and no doubt important to the defence of the country. Equally, however, he was aware that some found National Service very difficult, especially the men who were married and others posted to awful places and even to war zones.

Gerald Taylor

RAF 1952-54

In amongst the cards that arrived at Gerald's house on his 21st birthday was a brown envelope containing an invitation to join His Majesty's Air Force. Not the sort of coming-of-age present he would have wished for, but it was an invitation he could not refuse. The Air Ministry had lost no time in calling up this young man who had deferred his National Service so that he could complete a five-year apprenticeship as an electrical and refrigeration service engineer with his uncle's firm.

A few days later he arrived at RAF Padgate, near Warrington. "There," he wrote, "I spent a hectic time being kitted out, learning to march and being taught the difference between a Warrant and a Commissioned Officer." A week after that he was sent to RAF Wheeton, near Blackpool, where he did eight weeks basic training. A keen sports fan, he took the opportunity of being allowed out at weekends to go and watch the great Stanley Matthews playing. He also danced in the famous Tower Ballroom.

Gerald then went to RAF Melksham to train as an electrical mechanic, a trade for which his apprenticeship made him well suited. He took full advantage of the opportunities offered for sport, and was picked to play for the station cricket team. On completion of his course, he was posted to Germany, to 112 Squadron at RAF Jever. He soon settled into squadron life, and learned to service the electrics on the RAF's first jet fighters, the Meteor and the Vampire. For a short period at the beginning of 1953 he was based at RAF Butzwelerhof, near Cologne, where taxiing trials were taking place, and he was involved in solving problems with the undercarriage indicator lights.

Later that year Gerald and four other ground crew were sent to RAF

A Vampire at RAF Jever. The jet fighter was developed by the de Havilland Aircraft Company. It was the second jet fighter to be operated by the RAF, after the Gloster Meteor, and the first to be powered by a single jet engine. It was introduced in 1945 and retired from service in 1955.

Gerald Taylor, centre, with two of his pals.

Bruggen, a new station near the Dutch border. Here they set up a welcoming ground crew for the arrival of the squadron at the beginning of July. As more squadrons arrived it became a very busy, noisy station. A lot of flying went on at night as well as by day.

In August, Corporal Weatherby, who had given Gerald a good grounding in Vampire electrics, was recalled to the UK for a promotion course, and Gerald found himself in sole charge of the electrics on the station! Two weeks later, in Belgium on a NATO exercise, he was still in charge, no replacement NCO having been found. Clearly, he was regarded as sufficiently competent for this role, despite not being given the promotion that it warranted. He was issued with a three-ton Bedford mobile workshop and a large towing generator. This provided lights for the tents, and he took great delight in shutting it down without warning at 11pm! Gerald really enjoyed the experience of living and working under wartime conditions on exercises like this.

Though he held a UK driving licence, he was not a qualified lorry driver, but he been seen driving the Bedford, and was told to take a driving test back at Bruggen, which he passed, and so became a front line driver for the squadron. In October the squadron left Bruggen and headed for the French Zone, in the south west. Their destination was Friedrichshafen, on Lake Constance, and this meant an overnight stay en route at Heidelburg, the main base of the American Zone. Here the accommodation was luxurious in comparison to RAF quarters. Sadly, on the way they lost one of the lorries and two drivers when it went off the autobahn and into some trees. At Friedrichshafen they settled in well with their French counterparts, though the accommodation was inferior.

Gerald Taylor, working on a generator on exercise near Liege

After Christmas Gerald took a conversion course for the American Sabre fighter. He thought seriously about staying on, but decided against it because of family problems. He was demobbed in February 1954.

Many years later, Gerald saw an advertisement for a 112 Squadron reunion. Memories came flooding back of the trips he had done while in Germany: to Sylt, to Lake Constance, to Cologne, with its cathedral still standing amid the ruins, to Assen, in Holland, where he had seen the great Geoff Duke winning the 500cc Dutch TT on his Galera motorcycle. He decided to go, and has been every year since.

Gerald enjoyed his two years in the RAF. He had gained skills as an aircraft electrical mechanic, travelled extensively in Germany, played a lot of cricket and football, and maintained his association with the service through the squadron reunions and his involvement with the RAF Association (RAFA), of which he is a life member of his local Porthcawl branch.

Douglas Jones

Royal Army Ordnance Corps 1951-53

Douglas did not begin his National Service in the best of health, for he was suffering from a terrible cough on the day he left home. On the journey to Aldershot he drank his way through two bottles of medicine and when the train stopped at Reading he got out and bought two more! He felt absolutely rotten, but refused to report sick, and being a fit young man, he soon recovered.

Having driven a dairy van before being called up, Douglas was selected to be a driver in the Royal Army Ordnance Corps, the unit responsible for the supply of weapons, ammunition and all manner of equipment. He was posted to a mobile Motor Transport (MT) unit in Germany, where he drove the Bedford QL, delivering spares all over the country. He enjoyed driving on the autobahns, as motorways were unknown in Britain at that time. On one occasion he experienced the worst of the German winter. On a scheme on the East German border, he slept in the back of his lorry and woke up to find snow up to the tailboard! He eventually managed to dig his way out.

On another scheme he was in a forest at night when he saw what he took to be a light. Approaching with the utmost caution, expecting an attack from airborne troops, he was relieved to find that it was fungus on the side of the trees which was giving off a weird glow!

He later became a despatch rider, and unlike Norman Greening (qv) he rode a motor bike. One day he met an oncoming convoy. Trying to avoid it, he fell off his bike and, unseen by the driver, went under the first lorry. He emerged miraculously unhurt, but the bike wouldn't start, no matter how many time he tried. Finally he realised he hadn't cleared the hole in the filler cap. Once he had done that, it started straight away.

Douglas once fell foul of the Military Police. He was coming out of a chip shop, fish and chips in his hand, when unfortunately he ran into two MPs. Soldiers were forbidden to walk the street eating food, and he was put on a charge. He did not say whether he was allowed to finish his fish and chips!

The bad cough which Douglas suffered on his way to Aldershot was not his only medical problem. When he developed toothache he said to the dentist that he didn't want gas. However, he was given gas, and was in bed ill for the next four days. To make matters worse the dentist had, according to Douglas, "ripped my gum to pieces".

Another time an oncoming lorry hit his wing mirror and smashed it, leaving pieces of glass in Douglas's face. However, he managed to finish his service without any further mishaps.

Douglas had to spend the two years after his demob in the Emergency Reserve, and this involved attending training for two weeks each year. However, he was never called up again.

Norman Greening

Royal Corps of Signals 1949-51

Norman was a despatch rider, but rarely rode a motor bike. Instead he mostly travelled around Germany by train. Armed with Sten guns, he and a colleague travelled in pairs to the various destinations, including via the Soviet Zone to Berlin. They were only allowed to travel by night, getting what sleep they could, and only spent every fourth night in their own beds. Occasionally they dozed off and missed their stop, causing them to arrive back late, which resulted in a fine.

In many ways, being a despatch rider did not really seem like military life, much of the time being spent on trains. Because of the erratic hours they worked, they were only required to attend parades on their days off. They lived in requisitioned civilian houses in the town, and in their spare time played snooker in the YMCA or went swimming in the pool built by the Army.

Having completed a month's basic training at Catterick, Norman was the posted to Ripon, 25 miles to the south, for three months despatch rider training. The machine they rode was the heavy, rather rigid BSA, while their much envied corporal instructors had the marvellous Matchless machines. Norman was not new to motorcycling, having learned to ride his father's Norton. However, this required a

Norman Greening

different technique, as it had a sidecar, so it was not possible to lean over when cornering. Much of the practising was in the scenic North Yorkshire Moors, twenty or so riding in single file with an instructor to front and rear. On one occasion he recalls a man falling off and ending up covered in oil! On completion of the course Norman was posted to Bad Oeynhausen, the Headquarters of BAOR. The Royal Signals carried mail and messages to all four zones of occupation.

One of Norman's memories of Catterick was of a man who deserted after two weeks. When he was recaptured he was brought back and, in full public view, put through the standard Army punishment: marching endlessly up and down a hill, and being made to move coal from one area to another, then whitewashing the cleared area before moving the coal back over it. A pointless task but a deterrent to any who might have had thoughts of going absent without leave.

Norman looks back on his National Service as an education, and an opportunity to meet people from other parts of the country, including a man from Yorkshire who has remained a lifelong friend. It was, he says, a memorable time in his life, and he feels he made the most of it.

Donald Gerrard

The Welch Regiment 1955-57

Donald describes his National Service as "like the curate's egg, good in parts, but interspersed with long periods of boredom". Probably a view shared by many others who found it sometimes enjoyable, sometimes unpleasant, but overall a worthwhile experience.

Called up at 21 after three years studying for a history degree at Nottingham University, Donald was posted to Germany, where he did clerical work in the Motor Transport section. Determined to take full advantage of the travel opportunities offered by being located in central Europe, rather than going home on leave Donald spent his time visiting the Scandinavian countries that bordered with Germany: Denmark, Sweden and Norway. This was known as 'local leave' and was paid for by the Army. He had a fortnight in Copenhagen, where he acquired some Danish friends, and he visited Malmo and Oslo. This was before the era of affordable tourism, and would normally have been prohibi- tively expensive in those days. He also travelled extensively in Germany itself, visiting the Hartz Mountains and Berlin amongst other places.

He also visited the site of the former concentration camp at Belsen, which he describes as "an eerie and chastening experience. There seemed to be a deathly hush, not a sound, not even a bird singing".

Donald felt that many National Servicemen were given mundane tasks that were well below their intelligence level, simply because the Army did not know what to do with them. But when a new second in command decided that some of the NCOs had not had sufficient education, and set up classes for them, Donald, being one of the derided 'educated buggers', was given the challenging task of teaching English, and so that he had some authority he was promoted to corporal.

Donald once had to escort a man to the military prison in Bielefeld, a place which, in his words, "frightened me to death!" It certainly deterred him from ever considering breaching the Army's strict code of discipline. The punishment for the 'hard cases' that thought they could beat the system was a draconian regime which broke even the most recalcitrant offender.

David Llewelyn

South Wales Borderers 1960-63

David was among the very last men called up for National Service. In fact, as his call up papers did not arrive until he was 21, he thought he had been forgotten! Unlike others who were conscripted at this age, he was not completing an apprenticeship. Since leaving school he had been employed as a labourer in the quarry near his home village of St Brides Major, near Bridgend.

David decided to sign on for three years, so that he could enjoy the status and pay of a regular. Though he did not know it at the time, he would end up serving only three months more than those who had not chosen to do the third year, as they found themselves having to do an extra six months to meet the shortfall in manpower following the end of National Service, whereas David was demobbed three months early!

He did his basic training at Brecon Barracks. One advantage he had over his fellow recruits was that he was used to wearing boots at work, whereas others found it difficult to get used to them and suffered terrible blisters. Once training was over, David was posted as a Motor Transport driver to the SWB depot in Minden, where his job was mainly to drive officers around. He frequently drove the Austin Champ, which he considered a superior vehicle to the Land Rover.

He enjoyed the social life in the barracks, and as it was only a quarter of a mile from the town he had the choice of going into Minden for a night out. One thing he remembers about the town was the gigantic statue of the Kaiser. Despite the fact that he had led the country into a disastrous war, the local people still had sufficient respect for him not to pull it down afterwards.

David finished his service in a rather unfortunate way. He had reached the rank of corporal, but he got into a fight with a private soldier. He claimed that it was not his fault, but he was demoted. Had this not happened he might have stayed on in the Army, but instead he went back to his job in the quarry.

His attitude to National Service was that if you put your mind to it you could enjoy it and gain a great deal from it.

Gethyn Williams

REME 1955-57

Gethyn recalls the bliss of his first hot shower after two weeks in a German pine forest, when he was finally able to wash away the body odour that had built up during this time. The mobile showers that should have been available had never materialised, so he remained unwashed and increasingly smelly! It was not until he was back in barracks that he was able to get rid of the grime and pine needles.

Gethyn had been posted to Kunsbeck, a small village near Bielefeld, with the Royal Electrical and Mechanical Engineers, where his work was servicing everything from motorcycles to Chieftain tanks. In his second year he was moved to a light anti-aircraft company near Lippstadt. Here he looked after ten Ford lorries that towed the Bofors guns, two Austin Champs (large jeeps with Rolls Royce engines, pictured below), and the small engines fitted on each gun for charging the batteries to power their electric motors.

These small engines were started by pulling on a small rope. Sometimes the operator's hands would be painful and bleeding after repeatedly pulling the rope. The motors were very temperamental,

especially out on manoeuvres in bad weather. It helped if the spark plug was removed from the engine and warmed up in the flames of a small fire.

They worked alongside German mechanics, although there was little social contact with them. In fact, he became very aware during this time of a change in attitude when, in the mid-50s, the British ceased to be an Army of Occupation and became a Visiting Army, more concerned with the defence of West Germany than its post-war occupation. Suddenly British and American music was no longer played on the radio, and Allied military personnel now found themselves last in the queue in shops. It was not hostility so much as a change of attitude. Ten years had gone by since the end of the war, and the German people probably felt had now regained some self-respect.

However, the American influence was strong. Gethyn had his first drink of Coca Cola whilst on a two-week skiing course, and has never forgotten the taste of that first bottle! He also heard Bill Haley and his Comets for the first time, ushering in a new form of music that would dominate the next decade and beyond.

He enjoyed Lippstadt, and was part of a music group that entertained officers once a month. This is where his lifelong interest in music

began, with songs such as 'Old Man River', 'On the Street where You Live', and 'Sixteen Tons' as his solos.

An amusing but (to some) painful incident was when someone cleaning the toilets in the accommodation block had, deliberately or otherwise, rubbed caustic soda on the seats, causing severe burns to several posteriors!

Gethyn had been promoted to Corporal First Class, with the promise of becoming a sergeant if he signed on for a further five years, but he decided not to take up the offer. He describes the last six weeks of his National Service in Aldershot as 'a come down'. Now awaiting demob, he was no longer a corporal, and found it very irritating to be ordered around by junior NCOs to whom up till then he had been superior.

A Welsh-speaking farm boy, Gethyn had found National Service a shock at first, but he says, "It changed me dramatically; I became much stronger within myself". He had learned valuable lessons on handling authority; for example, that it was for more effective to control drunken men with patience and humour than with shouting and bullying.

Richard Tadman

Royal Armoured Corps 1951-53

Richard's memories of basic training have appeared earlier in the book. This is his account of his subsequent service:

We were eventually considered safe to be allowed onto a tank gunnery range, which entailed a journey to Warcop, in Cumbria, a more easy-going camp that was a pleasant change from Catterick. We were instructed in the use of the tank's 17 pounder gun, firing at the remains of tanks on the hillsides. When firing ceased we were taken to see the results of our shooting, and were amazed to see the many holes in the tank's armour. Our confidence was considerably shaken, as we had been led to believe that a tank was a safe thing to be in. This was the Army's way of telling us otherwise!

Eventually we were given a pass to go on leave. This involved a coach journey from Scotch Corner to London and a train ride to my home in

Maidstone, Kent. I only had a brief time with my family before returning to Victoria Coach Station to return to Catterick. Although nothing was said, I had a feeling that my family and friends had noticed a change in me, perhaps because I was constantly polishing my boots and calling my friends "'orrible little men"!

On completion of training I was posted to Tidworth to join the 17/21st Lancers. Known as 'The Death or Glory Boys' as a result of their famous Charge of the Light Brigade in the Crimean War, they had a long, proud history. Formerly a cavalry regiment, they had maintained their high military standards and unique traditions, one of which was that the cap badge, a striking silver skull and crossbones, was never called a badge, but a motto. If you called it a badge you were instantly and in no uncertain terms reminded what to call it!

From Tidworth I was posted to Munster, in Germany, where the regiment was stationed. We sailed overnight on the SS Empire Wansbeck, a vessel that clearly was not suited to holiday cruises, more like bruise cruises! The Catering Corps had prepared a fried bread and bacon supper, which ended up in bags thoughtfully provided by the ship's crew, who were obviously familiar with the weather in the North Sea! At the Hook of Holland we were transferred to a waiting train which took us to Munster. En route there were still ample reminders of the battles fought in the area a few years earlier. Munster, an industrial city, was still recovering from the destruction suffered during the war, and some of the more elderly citizens were not too pleased with our presence, still having memories of the conflict they had witnessed, and in some cases taken part in.

The regiment was equipped with the Centurion, the latest British tank, armed with a 20 pounder gun. The tanks were fully loaded with live rounds and were maintained to a high battle-ready standard. Training exercises were carried out at Sennelager, Soltau and Luneburg Heath and resulted in a high standard of tank handling. We had always to be aware of the Cold War, and the need to be ever prepared for an attack from the enemy on the other side of the border.

Being near Belsen at times, we were taken to see the notorious former Nazi concentration camp, something I shall never forget.

I think it would be right to say that National Service did us no harm. We went in as boys and came out as men, and, I'm sure, better and wiser citizens.

Richard Millington

Royal Army Service Corps 1960-63

Richard was one of the last recruits for National Service. He had deferred his call up so that he could complete his six-year apprenticeship as a fitter, and was 21 when he began his service in 1960. He had applied to join the Royal Electrical and Mechanical Engineers, where he could have employed his technical skills, but due to the Army's perverse selection methods he found himself instead in the Royal Army Service Corps. However, he was here able to employ another skill he had acquired before call up: the ability to drive buses. During his apprenticeship he had driven them in his spare time and held a PSV licence. It was a skill he was able to use to his advantage.

First, however, Richard had to get through six hard weeks of basic training. He recalls arriving at Aldershot station after a long day's travelling, and being marched the two miles to Blenheim Barracks in the dark, the man at the rear carrying a red light. He also recalls with amusement the Teddy Boys, rashly asserting that no army barber was going to ruin *their* hair styles, only to emerge in tears as years of lovingly cultivated quiffs lay on the floor, having been brutally whisked off by the barber's clippers in a matter of seconds! A far grimmer memory was of the two boys who hanged themselves, their finders hastily discharged. It was a tough time, not made any easier by the badly-cooked food. There were times when he asked himself, "What have we done to deserve this?" He associates Elvis Presley's 'Heartbreak Hotel' with this period. It seemed appropriate!

Life improved after passing out. Richard was posted to Yeovil for driver training, which, thanks to his civilian experience, he passed in six weeks. Then came a real stroke of luck. The Physical Recreation Unit required a driver to replace one who was being demobbed. This was really a civilian job, and he was not required to wear uniform when driving. He was paid two shillings and sixpence (12.5p) an hour, which nicely supplemented his meagre army pay, and he was excused normal army duties. During the fifteen months he was with this unit he was sometimes required to do other jobs, such as driving for MI5 in London, taking his passengers to top secret locations around the city. Needless to say, he was told nothing about the purpose of these journeys.

The Cuban missile crisis almost saw Richard on active service. He was told to be ready to board a Hercules transport aircraft, destination and purpose unknown, but the mission was cancelled. He returned to camp and the world breathed a sigh of relief that a nuclear holocaust had been averted. However, nuclear warfare still featured in Richard's life when he took part in exercises off the South Coast as duty driver, including visiting an underground nuclear bunker.

Just as the end of his two years was in sight he was told that he would have to serve an extra six months! The end of National Service had resulted in a manpower shortage, fewer volunteers having been recruited than were needed. So Richard's three remaining months became nine, and he found himself posted to Germany, to Hilden, some fifteen kilometres from Dusseldorf. Here he drove heavy transport all over the country, and was sometimes required to patrol the East German border, though without bullets in their guns. The Army was taking no chances! He found the German barracks considerably more comfortable than those in the UK. They slept four to a centrally heated room, the food was far better, and they had civilians to do the menial tasks such as cleaning. They also built their own club, paid for by the Amstel beer company and utilising the skills of the carpenters and other trades in the unit. They suspected that by having their lives made more comfortable they would be encouraged to stay on. Few were tempted; most wanted to get back to their civilian lives.

Richard noticed the contrast between the attitude of the German people in Hilden to the presence of British troops and that of those who lived close to the border. In Hilden he sensed resentment, especially among youths with neo-Nazi sympathies, and it was not felt to be safe to go out of the camp, whereas in the areas bordering on East Germany they were welcomed as defenders against the feared enemy on the other side of the barbed wire.

Despite having had to serve an extra six months on top of his two years, Richard enjoyed his time in the army, apart from the grim six weeks of basic training.

Overseas Postings
The Middle East

IN THIS SECTION I have grouped Cyprus, Egypt and Libya together, as National Servicemen were often moved from one to another of these countries in the course of their service.

Cyprus

This island, with its beach resorts, its mountain scenery, and its friendly people, is today a favourite holiday destination for millions of tourists. But in the 1950s, when it was a British Crown Colony, it was a place of danger and hostility. Its population, a mixture of Greeks and Turks, fought fiercely for control of the island, the Greeks wanting union with Greece, the Turks with Turkey. The British, for whom the island was a vital military and naval base, were having to use troops, including National Servicemen, to try to keep the peace between the two communities, as well as to combat the Greek-supporting EOKA terrorists, who were trying to drive them off the island.

It is a little known fact that no less than 781 British servicemen were killed during the four years of the Cyprus emergency (1955-59), as well as 15 civilian police officers. This was twice as many as those who died in the more recent Afghanistan conflict. A memorial stone honouring the dead was recently brought over from Cyprus and placed in the National Arboretum in Staffordshire. Cyprus was by no means a safe posting.

Egypt

Though not part of the Empire, Egypt had been under partial British control since the 1880s, mainly in the area of the Suez Canal. It remained so after the war, under the rule of King Farouk. However, during this time there was increasing resentment at the British presence in the country, which resulted in attacks on British service personnel. In 1952 Farouk was overthrown in a coup led by Colonel Abdel Nasser, who, in 1956, nationalised the Suez Canal. This was not an illegal act, but it roused fears that a vital trade route to the Far East could be cut off, and the response was an invasion by the joint forces of Britain, France and Israel. However, the USA refused to support it, seeing it as a colonialist venture, and British Prime Minister Anthony Eden was forced to make a humiliating withdrawal. Many National Servicemen were among the forces sent on this abortive mission, some even being involved in brief skirmishes before the operation was called off.

Libya

Colonised by Italy in 1931 and liberated by the Allies in 1943 , Libya was an independent state ruled by King Idris. However, Britain retained a strong military presence there in return for economic subsidies, as it was an important military transit route across the Middle East. British forces were withdrawn in 1966, and in 1969 Idris was overthrown by Colonel Gaddafi. Unlike in Egypt and Cyprus, there was no resentment of the British among the population, and it was regarded as a safe and pleasant posting.

Doug Jones

Royal Marines 1956-58

One of those who had the thankless task of fighting terrorists in Cyprus was Marine Doug Jones, from Kenfig Hill.

Leaving school at 18, Doug deferred his National Service in order to go to Aberystwyth University, but he found it unappealing and left after two terms. A period of casual work filled the gap until he received his call-up papers and chose, on the recommendation of a friend, to go into the Marines. He was selected for officer training and spent four months

Doug Jones (left, standing) on patrol in the Troodos Mountains, Cyprus

at Eaton Hall, but to his intense disappointment he was not commissioned. No reason was given for this, which perhaps made it worse. However, he then trained with 40 Commando at Lympstone, in Devon, a tough course which included cliff climbing, assault courses, abseiling, unarmed combat and landing in small boats. He also played rugby and went cross-country running. Being young, fit and energetic, Doug did not find the regime daunting. In fact, he enjoyed it.

His training completed, he was posted overseas, first to Malta, then to Libya for desert training, and finally to Cyprus, where, as stated earlier, the British forces were trying, not very successfully, to keep the peace between the Greeks and the Turks. Doug's unit was in the Pathos Forest, up in the mountains, where it was relatively safe, though they could be ambushed at any time. He soon realised that the local people were always one step ahead of the British. Shepherds would call to one another when a daytime patrol was spotted, and even at night they seemed to know exactly where the soldiers were.

Doug recalls arriving in a village one pitch black night. The only light came from the tavern, and when the patrol went in, having made a stealthy approach, five cups of coffee were lined up on the bar ready for them!

One task which Doug disliked intensely was having to search people's houses, and he was always impressed by the tolerance and courtesy of the inhabitants. They knew the British were there to protect them, yet at the same time were foreign intruders. Sometimes he had to arrest suspects, and he recalls the distressing sight of women and children screaming because their men were being taken away. He particularly disliked the policemen from the civilian Special Branch, who were rumoured to beat suspect up in the cells.

One tactic was to throw a cordon round a particular area at dusk and then set up ambushes within it. Troops from several regiments encircled an area of rough terrain with the aim of containing, capturing or indeed killing terrorists who were thought to be hiding in that area and launching attacks from there. Doug's unit was part of the cordon but they also went into the encircled area at night to lay ambushes.

Returning in the half light at dawn, they sometimes had to cross the cordon at points manned by the troops of other regiments, who would not necessarily have known that Doug's unit had gone in to the area at dusk, and there was always the fear that they would wake from a doze, see armed men approaching and open fire. Fortunately, that never happened.

There were usually half a dozen men on these incursions, and they were not normally officer led. On one occasion, however, they were accompanied by writer and journalist Auberon Waugh, a second lieutenant in another regiment. They found his methods unorthodox. Becoming separated from the patrol, he was found wandering alone and laying an ambush on white rocks in bright moonlight, which seemed unwise, to say the least!

Doug greatly enjoyed his National Service, and considered signing on at the end, but decided on balance that the life of a regular soldier was not for him. He enjoyed the comradeship and the mutual trust in working in a small unit, and felt he had gained personally from meeting men from all backgrounds. Although he had not been successful in seeking a commission, he felt he had benefited from the course and the lessons in leadership he had learned, and the commando training had developed him both physically and mentally.

Rex Chess

Royal Engineers 1957-59

Like Doug Jones (q.v.), with whom he grew up in Kenfig Hill, near Porthcawl, Rex spent most of his National Service in Cyprus, although the two men never met there, as Rex was based in the port of Famagusta while Doug operated in the Troodos Mountains, and Rex, unlike Doug, did not come into contact with terrorists. As skipper of a landing craft, his job involved taking supplies to British and American ships moored in the harbour, and helping with civilian trade. Famagusta, a busy harbour, was sometimes full, but the shallow draft of the landing craft enabled it to land goods on the nearby beaches. He also landed incoming army units in this way, as the harbour was often too crowded to allow in troopships.

Landing Craft Tank (LCT) Mk8; a WW2 assault craft of the type involved in the invasion of the Suez canal.

Rex therefore saw very little active service, his one memory of conflict being of an occasion when terrorists opened fire on a group of soldiers' wives in the town, and then disappeared. Most of the fighting he witnessed was between rival regiments of the British Army! To avoid this conflict, the men of the Royal Ulster Rifles and the men of the Welsh Regiment had to have time off on alternate weekends.

Called up at 18, Rex recalls the ritual humiliation of basic training at Great Malvern, followed by fourteen weeks' training with the Royal Engineers, where he learned to skipper a landing craft. These vessels were designed to carry troops to the enemy beaches, but they could also transport three Centurion tanks or eleven loaded lorries. However, as they were not required for this purpose in Cyprus, where Rex was posted on completion of his training, they were, as stated earlier, used as supply vessels. In an attempt to show even-handedness to the rival communities, one craft was crewed with Greeks, the other with Turks, but the two crews never interacted.

A frightening incident occurred one evening when Rex was taking his Greek crew home in a lorry. This was not normally his job, but the regular driver was ill. Guarded by a soldier with a sub machine gun, he was driving through a notoriously dangerous village when he skidded and knocked one of the front wings off. The impact caused all the electrics to fail, and the vehicle ground to a halt. In an ominous silence, punctuated by the barking of a dog, Rex somehow managed to find a way to reconnect the ignition cables. To his immense relief, the engine restarted, and he drove on at high speed!

Rex had plenty of time for off-duty enjoyment. Relations with the Navy were cordial, and the troops were often invited on board ship to watch films, as well as to shower and have meals. Sometimes they dived off a platform on the side of a ship, a drop of some forty feet. So clear was the water that before diving, a heavy object such as a nut and bolt had to be thrown into it so that the splash could indicate where the surface was. They were occasionally taken on unofficial trips to other ports, such as Beirut. On one of these times they came across gun runners, whom they frightened off by firing flares across their bows!

Rex very much enjoyed his time in the Army, and considered

applying for a commission, but his mother's illness required him to come home. He had a great respect for the regular soldiers, and recalls one occasion, when, after some bullets of his had been stolen, one of the regulars forced the culprit to return them through a little not very gentle persuasion! He noted that, ironically, men from public school backgrounds were more inclined to mix and were less class-conscious than others, as well as adapting more easily to being away from home.

He felt that the Army offered a great deal of support to young men, in terms of health, education and social development. There were numerous opportunities to gain qualifications that were transferable into civilian life, and for this reason he felt that National Service was a valuable experience. Personally he felt that he came out a far more mature individual than when he had gone in.

Huw Rees

The Welch Regiment 1957-59

Despite serving overseas for most of his National Service, Huw felt that he never really left Wales, such was the family spirit within the Welch Regiment, to which he was called up in April 1957. His basic training at Maindy Barracks, in Cardiff, followed by riot training at Worcester, was completed relatively quickly, for his unit was urgently needed in Cyprus to combat the EOKA terrorists.

Inevitably in a terrorist campaign, innocent civilians were drawn into the conflict, but Huw never felt that the ordinary Greek Cypriot people were antagonistic towards the British. Indeed, some looked upon them as protectors from the Turks. Children would approach the camp guards to exchange eggs for chocolate, but if they did not appear one morning that was a sign that an attack was about to take place. It was not indiscriminate killing, however. Soldiers were targeted, but not their families, and when on one occasion two sergeants' wives were gunned down from a passing car (Rex Chess also referred to this incident), it caused an outcry from military and civilians alike. Huw was twice shot at but was unhurt on both occasions.

Huw was a radio operator in the Signals Platoon. Messages were frequently sent in code, but the one that would have flummoxed any eavesdropping enemy was the one that he once sent in Welsh! On this occasion a top secret message that a unit of the Special Branch of the British civilian police, (who worked alongside their military colleagues) was going out on patrol had to be sent urgently. It would have taken too long to get the keys to the cupboard where the code books were kept, and knowing that Wally from Llandeilo, the man who would receive the message, was, like himself, a Welsh speaker, Huw obtained permission to send it in that language. It was probably the most unconventional message he ever sent.

One of his more unusual duties was "Guard Commander of the Salvation Army Wives Home!" Many men had been separated from their families in Cyprus for long periods, and the Salvation Army set up a home for wives in Benghazi so that they could spend time with their husbands. They were not in any way under the control of the army, but the army appreciated this service and made sure the women were well guarded.

From Cyprus Huw was posted on to Benghazi, where he arrived just before Christmas 1958. Here, for the next four months, they trained in the desert, glad to be away from the tensions and dangers of life in Cyprus.

Huw completed his National Service in April 1959. He returned to his home town of Kenfig Hill and resumed his job as a forestry worker. However, in 1962 came the Cuban Missile Crisis, and as he had not yet completed his time as a reservist he was liable to be called up again. He actually received two letters on the same day, one instructing him to report to the barracks in Cardiff for resumption of service, and another telling him to ignore the previous letter, as his services were not, after all, required, much to his relief.

What Huw chiefly remembers about his National Service was the comradeship, which has continued all through his life. Every year he and some former comrades have met in Cardiff Rugby Club, though sadly only six of the fourteen are now left.

Paul Hatcham

Royal Artillery 1954-57

Another man who was lucky to survive terrorist attacks in Cyprus was Paul Hatcham. While driving a ten ton lorry, he was about to cross a small bridge when suddenly everything seemed to go into slow motion as the vehicle was rocked by a massive explosion. It had hit an anti-personnel mine. He and his two guards, miraculously unhurt, dived into a ditch and lay there for a few minutes, but their attackers had run off. Once it was safe, they changed the damaged wheel and continued on their journey.

On another occasion, as he stood in the queue for the latrine, a shot rang out, followed by a scream, and a man slumped to the ground. He had been the target of a sniper, who had fired indiscriminately into the crowd and then disappeared. These hit-and-run attacks were the common tactics of the terrorists, designed to undermine the morale of the British soldiers, whom many regarded as a hated occupying force, even though they were in Cyprus to try to keep the peace.

Paul's journey to Cyprus was via Egypt, where he was sent in 1956 as part of the ill-fated invasion force. Such was the speed of the British withdrawal that they had hardly set foot on Egyptian soil before they were re-embarking for an unknown destination. It was not until they had landed in Cyprus that they learned where they were - by asking a group of children!

Paul had learned to drive before being called up, and this became his job in the army, handling all types of vehicle

Paul Hatcham, studio portrait

from lorries to Land Rovers. It was in one of the latter that he fell foul of the strict army dress regulations. He was coming back from leave, but due to an unforeseen change in train times he arrived at camp with only twenty minutes to spare. His relief changed to horror when he discovered that he was duty driver for church parade at 0800, leading the convoy, accompanied by the Regimental Sergeant Major. Because of the cold weather, the radiator of the Land Rover had been drained off the previous night, and Paul only just had time to part-fill it from a fire bucket. It was not enough, and as they made their way to the church, steam began to seep ominously out of the engine.

He managed to reach their destination, and as soon as possible drove behind the village hall so that he could attend to the dangerously overheated engine. Clouds of steam were by now billowing out. Knowing that the filler cap would be red hot, Paul used his beret to protect his hand as he gingerly unscrewed it. With a loud bang, the cap and the beret shot into the air. The beret landed on top of a roof, well out of reach. He managed to retrieve the cap and find water for the radiator, but he knew that he would be in deep trouble for having lost his beret. Sure enough, when the RSM got into the Land Rover his first question was "Where's your cap, soldier?" Paul had to confess to its loss, and was ordered to report to the RSM at 0700 the next morning, where he was given a week's 'jankers'. He had paid a heavy price for his late arrival from leave.

A far more serious offence was losing one's rifle. One of Paul's duties in Cyprus was to collect water every day. He and the two guards who routinely accompanied him stopped at an orange plantation to fill up, and one of the guards left his rifle in the cab when they got out to stretch their legs. Suddenly he realised what he had done, but when he got back to the vehicle, the rifle had gone. The local people all stared at the floor when asked who had taken it, and even threats with a brandished Sten gun had no effect. The guard was put under close arrest, and both he and Paul faced a court martial. Paul was exonerated, but the man was sentenced to 156 days' hard labour, such was the seriousness of the offence. He returned a broken man, his weight having dropped from thirteen stone to eight. Some months later, after an attack on a village in an attempt to catch terrorists, one man admitted taking the rifle, but it was never returned.

Another frightening experience for Paul was being ordered to enter a building where the enemy might be hiding. This happened on a night patrol, and it was Paul, not the officer in charge, who had to kick the door open and go in. Terrified, he crept in, but fortunately the place was empty. Paul was unimpressed by the conduct of the officer, who had hidden himself after ordering Paul to put his life at risk!

After a year in Cyprus, Paul returned home. The ship encountered stormy seas, which battered it for 36 hours, and everyone was violently sick. The captain, who never actually appeared, sent a bottle of gin down to the four soldiers. 90% proof, it was like drinking petrol, but it at least took their minds off their nausea.

Paul did three years' service, the extra year entitling him to better pay. He had found leaving home traumatic, but felt that he had enormously gained in confidence and self-reliance at the end of his National Service.

Conrad Hawes

Parachute Regiment 1954-56

It was almost unprecedented for a working class boy from Maesteg to become an officer during National Service, but Conrad Hawes was an exception. He did have one big advantage, however; he had previously served as an officer in the Merchant Navy.

Conrad had lost his father at the age of six, but nevertheless his mother had been determined that he and his brother should have the best education possible. He won a scholarship to grammar school, where he was been an exceptional scholar, but at the age of sixteen he was lured by a Merchant Navy poster offering the chance to see the world. To the fury of both his mother and his headmaster, he left school and went to sea as an apprentice. Two years later he was promoted to Third Officer, which meant that for eight hours a day he was in sole charge of the ship, a huge respon- sibility for a lad still in his teens.

However, after four years he decided to come ashore, mainly because he could see how his fellow officers hated the separa- tion for long periods from their wives and families. He was still single, but he did not want to be similarly affected after he mar- ried. It was not an easy decision; he had travelled all round the world, and it had been a great education for leadership. He had earned the respect of a rough and ready Liverpudlian crew.

Conrad Hawes, studio portrait

Having left the Merchant Navy, he was no longer exempt from National Service, and he applied for the Army. He was sent to a basic training unit in Devon, where, during the first week, he was taken aside and told he was playing rugby for the unit team that Saturday. This unexpected selection was purely as a result of his being Welsh! He scored two tries, so was off to a good start.

"There followed eleven weeks of basic training," he wrote, "mainly marching up and down. Our drill sergeant was only about five feet tall, but he made up for that with his screaming voice. He had a lot of trouble with me at the start. Because I had been at sea for four years, when I walked on land my body swayed from side to side. He did not like this. It looked even worse when I carried a rifle."

Conrad's rolling gait did not prevent him from being selected for officer training. At the Potential Officers Unit they were given tasks and problems to display leadership skills. "My four years at sea could not have prepared me better for this. I was promoted to Leading PO and wore a special badge." Out of the initial intake of thirty, he was one of only two selected to attend Eaton Hall Officer Cadet School for four months' training. "Eaton Hall was like a finishing school. The officers

Group of officer cadets and instructors outside Eaton Hall,
Conrad Hawes on back row, extreme left

and NCOs were first class. They made you feel good about yourself."

However, it proved to be very difficult to find a regiment to be commissioned into. National Service officers were not wanted, because they were there for such a short time. Some regiments did not see them as 'proper' officers because they had not done the two years' training of regular officers. However, Conrad's rugby skill came to his rescue. A paratroop officer who played on the wing offered to introduce him to his regiment. He was accepted on condition that he passed the Parachute Course.

"The 'P' Course," wrote Conrad, "was a physical endurance test every soldier had to pass before entry into the Parachute Regiment. Officers and other ranks competed together. I found out later that 75% of students failed the course. Officers wore striped rugby jerseys, while other ranks had numbers on their backs. I remember one game called 'Murderball' played with a heavy medicine ball. I picked up the ball and was then lifted by a few soldiers and thrown against the wall bars, which resulted in two black eyes. A lot of soldiers failed the 'Tarzan' swing on a rope over the centre of the gym where a six foot high work-horse stood. You had to let go at the last moment to clear the horse. A lot of men would not let go for fear of landing on their backs across the horse. They immediately failed the course. I remember having to box one round with a man my own weight. I was so scared I rushed at him with fists flying and knocked him out of the ring! After lots more tests I passed the course and was sent to Abingdon for parachute training."

"GO!" was all I kept hearing for the next few days as I jumped, first off a 2 foot bench, then 4 foot, 6 foot, 12 foot platform with harness, 24 foot, 36 foot, then from a basket under a balloon using a parachute for the first time. Then I was climbing aboard an aircraft knowing that at the next "GO!" I would have to jump for real.

"Jumping from a plane was not so bad. There was strong discipline and lots of checks. We jumped in sticks of eight men. You hooked your strap on to the rail above and the chap behind you checked it was secure. When you left the plane you flew back in the slipstream, the strap pulling out the parachute from the pack on your back. You then glided to the ground, where you pressed your legs together and rolled over on impact.

"On one occasion I had a frightening experience. The strings of my parachute became entangled and the chute did not open. I was hurtling towards the ground. I was about to open my reserve chute when the main one finally opened, only just in time for me to land safely. Although I had jumped last in the stick of eight men, I was first on the ground, much to their surprise!

"After a pleasant two weeks in the RAF Officers' Mess I had my airborne wings sewn on my uniform and my Second Lieutenant's pips on my shoulders, ready to join the First Battalion the Parachute Regiment."

The Regiment was stationed in Cyprus, just outside Nicosia. Conrad was put in charge of No 1 Platoon of A Company, which consisted of a sergeant, three corporals and forty men. Their duties were mainly policing the villages and towns and patrolling the mountains and forested areas of Northern Cyprus in search of terrorists. It was potentially dangerous work. On one occasion a bomb was thrown from the window of a house onto a jeep passing below. A major in the jeep was very badly injured. Conrad was ordered to "go up there and sort them out so they won't want to do it again". He took forty armed paratroopers and, on the pretence of searching for arms, went into every house and ransacked it "coldly in front of weeping women and dumb-founded children… We found no arms. The scene has haunted me ever since".

Despite having to do unpleasant jobs like that, there was plenty of enjoyment to be had on Cyprus. Conrad played rugby and was in the Parachute Regiment team that won the Cyprus Sevens, which included two Welsh internationals, Alan Pask and Haydn Morgan. There were beaches nearby and swimming pools in the hotels and sports clubs. "Living in a tented officers' mess was like living in a luxury hotel." Like all officers, he enjoyed the privilege of having a personal servant, known as a batman.

Inevitably, Conrad was sometimes made aware of the contrast between his background and that of the majority of his fellow officers, mainly ex-public school boys. He had a double disadvantage of being not only working class, but Welsh, and on one occasion was introduced to the officers' mess with the words "Taffy was a Welshman, Taffy was a thief". However, he was sufficiently self-confident to deal with such tactless jibes, and on the whole got on well with the other officers. Surviving the 'P' Course had given them a common bond that transcended class barriers.

An interesting experience for Conrad was the week he spent on an exchange with the French Army, who were also in Cyprus. Despite his schoolboy French, he had a great time. "Every meal in the officers' mess was a party. The red wine flowed!" He did a parachute jump (where he nearly forgot to hook up), at the end of which there were 27 casualties. Walking round the camp later, he came across half a dozen paratroopers buried up to their necks in the ground, a punishment for refusing to jump from the plane during the exercise!

The ill-fated invasion of Egypt to reclaim the Suez Canal took place in September 1956, and in preparation the regiment was flown back to the UK to practise a parachute jump as they had not done one for some time. Conrad's platoon was flown back to Cyprus in a wartime Lancaster bomber. He sat in the nose gunner's cockpit and enjoyed a panoramic view.

As Conrad and his platoon boarded the huge landing craft at Famagusta Harbour, they knew they were going to war. This was not an exercise, this was real. The men had given him letters to their wives and girlfriends, some of which he had helped to write. They crossed the calm sea, but as they approached the coast they were told there would be no enemy waiting for them. They would not have to wade through the sea on landing, waiting to be picked off. Once on the beach at Port Said they dug into the sand.

As it became light there were sporadic bursts of fire striking the sand around them but there were no casualties. They were ordered to move through the empty streets of the town towards their objective, the Suez Canal, but half way through the day the order came to stand down. They marched back to the docks and boarded the aircraft carrier Ark Royal. So as not to give the impression of a humiliating withdrawal, they lined the decks wearing their red berets, but there were no spectators to witness their departure. When they arrived back in Aldershot they had a Welcome Home parade through the town and Conrad had the honour of carrying the Regimental Colours.

Conrad found life rather dull in Aldershot, and by then he had met his future wife, so when his National Service came to an end he decided to leave, even though he was offered a three-year regular commission. He was a capable officer, but he hated the idea of killing. He knew also that he would at times have to be brutal, as in the incident in Cyprus when he had been ordered to ransack people's homes. He had enjoyed the physical side of army life, especially in the Parachute Regiment, and he had enjoyed life in the Officers' Mess. He was relieved not to have had to go to war.

So in 1956 he resigned his commission and went back into civilian life, having packed a wealth of experience into the previous six years.

Llew Williams

Royal Army Medical Corps 1945-48

Llew Williams was called up on 30th Octoberr 1945, so strictly speaking he did not do National Service in the generally understood meaning of the term, i.e. a fixed period of service. What Llew did was really War Service, even though the war had ended three months earlier, but his enlistment was 'for the duration', in other words, until such time as the Army no longer required him.

It was not until 1948 that National Service for a fixed term of eighteen months (later two years) was introduced. So when Llew received his call-up papers, he had no idea for how long he was going to serve. In the event, it was two and a half years.

In some ways, Llew was better prepared for the ordeal of initiation into the Army than most of the other eighteen-year-olds around him. For a start, he was used to living away from his home in Rhydymain, Meirionnydd, having left it at the age of fifteen to become a civilian clerk with the Police in Caernarvon. He was accustomed to a disciplined environment in which orders had to be obeyed and superiors respected. He was used to looking smart at all times. His feet were hardened to boots, which he had worn as a schoolboy in Rhydymain, so he did not suffer from blisters. Not for him the tears in the night of homesick boys trying to come to terms with this harsh, alien world.

Llew was sent for basic training to Ballykinlar Barracks, on the shores of Dundrum Bay in County Down, Northern Ireland. Here, for thirteen weeks, he and his fellow recruits were put through the painful process of being turned into soldiers, being shouted at and drilled from morning till night. Meal breaks provided respite, but the food was unpalatable, yet, here again, Llew was at an advantage. Having lived in lodgings since leaving home, he was used to food that fell below the standard of his mother's cooking. In between the square bashing he ran over the sand dunes in PT kit, threw grenades, fired rifles and sat intelligence tests to determine where he would be sent for the rest of his service.

It was decided that Williams 431 was a bright lad but lacked the qualities required of an infantryman, being unable, in his own words,

Llew Williams
(kneeling, right) and
RAMC pals in Egypt

"to hit a barn door from ten yards" with a rifle, nor to throw a grenade far enough away to avoid being hit by a shower of mud as it exploded! So he was sent to train as a Medical Orderly at the RAMC Depot near Fleet, Surrey. Here he studied everything from the human skeleton through First Aid, casualty evacuation to the correct way to make a hospital bed. After three months he was designated Medical Orderly Class 3.

From here Llew was sent to the British Military Hospital at Wheatly, near Oxford, which specialised in head injuries. The principal surgeon was a German Jew who had come to Britain to escape the Nazis, one of hundreds of gifted men whose talents had been lost to Germany thanks to Hitler's insane racial policies. Here Llew's duties were mainly clerical. He did a course in medical terminology so that when he took notes from the doctors he had a basic understanding of their vocabulary and the ability to decipher their handwriting!

His next posting, which he chose because it was not too far from home, was Chester Military Hospital, where he spent four months. Then he received notice that he was to be posted overseas.

His destination was the Canal Zone in Egypt, which at that time was still governed by Britain. However, presumably because normal shipping routes had been disrupted by the war, his route was overland through France and then across the Mediterranean from Toulon. So after a brief embarkation leave, Llew crossed from Dover to Calais. Here, for the first time since 1939, he was able to enjoy good food. After five years of the grey-brown wartime bread of Britain, he could now savour the taste of real white bread. The French may have been short of food during the German Occupation, but now it seemed to be plentiful.

They journeyed by train, on uncomfortable wooden seats, all the way down to Toulon, where, even though they were now in the South of France, it was bitterly cold. This was January 1947, the beginning in Britain of the worst winter of the century, and they had to hang around for a week waiting for a ship, often walking the streets to try to keep warm. Once aboard, they had to learn a new skill: sleeping in a hammock! They were taught the technique of folding one's blankets in such a way that it made an envelope, and it was a surprisingly comfortable bed once one had manoeuvred oneself into it. However, as the ship entered a warmer climate the cabin became very stuffy, and Llew and a few others decided to sleep in the open air. However, they had to be up early before the crew arrived with mops and buckets to swab the decks.

Landing at Port Said was quite an experience for a country lad from North Wales, hearing a new language, seeing people dressed in strange clothes, the women covered from head to foot with only their eyes visible. They were besieged by beggars, who were sent away, politely or otherwise, by the old soldiers who had served there previously. They stayed at the RAMC depot in El Balah for a week or so before being sent by local train to Cairo, where they were to report to GCHQ of Middle East Land Forces. However, when they arrived they were told that GCHQ had moved to El Fayid, on the Bitter Lakes. From here Llew was posted to Moascar, a hospital for the families of British servicemen, where he became the secretary to the obstetrics specialist. It was very hot during the day, sometimes 120 degrees Fahrenheit, but at night the temperature could drop to below freezing point. This resulted in the deaths through pneumonia of several babies whose mothers had not kept them warm enough at night.

There were other health hazards, too. Llew wrote, "The daily life, the habits and customs in Egypt were a complete contrast to my life in Wales, and there was a total indifference to the rules of ordinary hygiene. We as British servicemen were isolated from these dangers in our camps, but when we went out of camp care had to be exercised. After about six months we were starkly reminded of this when cholera broke out in the Nile Delta due to a botched sewage system. All servicemen and those natives who worked in the hospital and kitchens were inoculated with an anti-cholera vaccine. Rumour has it that 250,000 Egyptians died in the epidemic but not one servicemen."

Llew became Chief Clerk to the hospital and was promoted to Corporal. He could have become a Sergeant if he had agreed to sign on for a further twelve months, but he decided that two and a half years in the Army was long enough.

The return journey was by sea all the way this time, stopping at Malta and Gibraltar before passing through the notoriously rough Bay of Biscay. Unlike most of his colleagues, Llew was not seasick but certainly felt uncomfortable and was pleased when the ship docked at Liverpool. From there he went by train to the demob centre in York, where he was given the regulation civilian clothing before returning to Merioneth and his career as a police officer, which he began on 30th June 1948.

John Miskill

Royal Army Ordnance Corps 1952-54

Of all the men I interviewed, John was the only one who said he had hated National Service! For him, it had not been a happy experience, especially basic training. While this was a hard time for most men, it seems to have been particularly unpleasant for John. He describes it as "being treated like a nincompoop" and "a sentence for something you had not done". He hated the utter disrespect shown to the recruits, such as having their mail thrown onto the floor while being given out, so that it got wet, leaving the letter indecipherable. He hated the inedible food, served up by uncaring cooks. He hated the idiotic rules that windows in the prison-like barrack rooms be kept half open at night, even in the coldest weather, and that stoves remain unlit so that they did not have to be cleaned. He recalls waking up one morning to see a layer of snow, blown in through the open window, on the bed of the man next to him! Indeed, the behaviour of the NCOs in this particular camp seems to have verged on the sadistic. They would, for example, alter the water temperature in the showers from freezing to boiling while the men were under them.

There were other practices, too, some of them criminal. Deductions were made from their niggardly pay of fourteen shillings a week to cover non-existent barrack room damages. A man would find one of his blankets missing, apparently stolen, so the NCOs would make the seemingly kindly suggestion that the others 'chip in two shillings each to buy him a replacement so that he did not get into trouble.' The NCOs would pocket the money and replace the blanket which had mysteriously disappeared.

Life became a little easier when John was posted to Egypt, where he spent a year in Fayid, in the Suez Canal Zone, close to the Great Bitter Lake. Food was marginally better, the discipline a little more relaxed. His civilian trade was repairing boots, and he was promoted to corporal i/c the boot repair unit, a job which no doubt, this being the army, kept him busily occupied! However, life was far from pleasant. They could not leave the camp for fear of being attacked by anti-British terrorists, and within the camp there were regular outbreaks of dysentery due to poor hygiene. The water in the oil drums in which they had to wash their plates was usually dirty, as were the hands of the cooks who served up the food. It was normal for an officer to come into the mess to ask "Any complaints?" and equally normal for this question to be met with complete silence, but on one occasion John decided to stand up and complain about the dirty conditions and the awful food. The officer took no notice whatsoever. That was also usual.

From Egypt John went to Famagusta, in Cyprus. Here there was (at that time) no terrorist problem; the only people who accosted them were the prostitutes, who charged ten shillings a time for their services. As John did not wish to contract venereal disease, which might have resulted in prolonging his service, he did not take up their offers. Now able to go off camp, they went to the nearby beaches and to the open air cinema, or would go off riding on hired bicycles. They also went to night clubs, but had to be wary of the girls, who tended to disappear at the end of the night, having relieved them of their money! The food in camp was still not great, but at least on his corporal's pay John could afford to eat out sometimes.

He recalls a couple of dramatic incidents. One night he saw the beginnings of a fire in one of the tents. Instinctively, he ran inside and pulled out a man who was in a state of shock. The next morning, on parade, he was publicly commended for his prompt action. A minute or two later, it would have been impossible to enter the blazing tent and the man would have lost his life. John found this praise embarrassing; he felt he had only done the same as anyone else in the circumstances. On another occasion he was on duty in the guard house armed with a Sten gun. He was told to guard a man who had broken into camp, presumably to try to steal weapons. When the man made for the door, John was reluctant to fire the gun, not knowing where the bullets would go in this confined space, so he hit him on the chest with his gun. The man fell to the floor and made no further attempts to escape.

John left the Army feeling it had done nothing for him other to build up a mass of resentment. He still faced the possibility of being recalled, and so great was his fear of this that for years afterwards he was haunted by a dream in which an Arab worker in the recruiting office gave him an application form to fill in, and when he had done so, placed it in a pile. John then walked out of the office, but immediately turned round and went back in, retrieved the form from the pile and tore it up! Much to his relief he was not recalled, even during the 1956 Suez Crisis, though had this gone on longer than a few days he might well have been.

Brian Johnson

Royal Army Service Corps 1954-56

One afternoon in Egypt, Brian heard an unusual announcement over the tannoy. "Will all personnel please get into their lorries? Make sure doors and windows are locked, and stay in your vehicles until further notice." Within minutes a vast black cloud appeared in the sky. It was not rain, but a swarm of locusts! "It was," recalls Brian, "like a scene straight out of the Bible." Within an hour they had all eaten and either died or flown away. No grass, no flowers, no canvas was left. Thousands of dead covered the ground, and it took three days to clear the mess. Brian had witnessed something he would never see again, and it remains one of the most vivid memories of his National Service.

Brian began six weeks basic training in May 1954 in Blandford, Dorset. It was not far from Poole, where they spent any free time at weekends on the beach. They experienced the usual bullying from the NCOs, but managed to get their own back on two of the corporals by tying them to their beds on the morning they left the camp. It was rare that such acts of insubordination went unpunished, but on this occasion they got away with it!

They were flown out to Egypt in a Dakota transport plane. They made a refuelling stop in Malta after a bumpy ride, and as they landed a familiar voice behind Brian said "This is the last bloody time I will ever go up in one of these buckets!" It was none other than actor and comedian Terry-Thomas, presumably on his way to do a show for the troops.

They flew on to Egypt, which Brian describes as "a wonderful country." Their camp was in Moasca, and it was there that they witnessed the swarm of locusts. Over the coming months they had a trip to Cairo, where they saw the Pyramids and the Casbah. Brian enjoyed sport and had plenty of opportunities to play rugby for the Company, and also water polo, in which he competed in the 1956 final at St Paul's Bay, Malta. Unfortunately his team lost!

A chance encounter in a cinema in Egypt brought Brian into unexpected contact with a hitherto unknown relation by marriage. He found himself sitting next to a Welshman, and got into conversation with him.

"Where are you from?" he asked

"Port Talbot" replied Brian.

"Oh" said the man. "My sister got married last week to a boy from Port Talbot. Chris Johnson. Do you know him?"

"I should do" said Brian. "He's my brother!"

The name of his new brother-in-law was Roger Price, and the two subsequently became good friends, both playing rugby for Kenfig Hill.

Brian's first encounter with danger came when they had to transport some Welsh Guards to Cyprus in flat bottom boats and the take them up into the Troodos Mountains, where they were likely to encounter EOKA terrorists. Brian was convoy leader, being a corporal at this time, and rode about a mile ahead on his motor bike, looking out for suspicious activity. He suddenly noticed about ten men on rocks looking down at the road, and at the same time he saw that the sign to the Troodos Mountains had been changed and was pointing to the right. He turned back and reported to an officer, who ordered them to ignore the sign and keep left. Nobody was to stop and guns were to be kept at the ready. They got through safely, but could well have been led into an ambush had they followed the signs.

Brian next found himself in Tripoli, the capital of Libya. Here he spent a very pleasant last six months of his service. There was plenty of sport every day, and their only duties were guarding the officers' families on their private beach! During this time they were comfortably accommodated in the rooms above the company bakery.

Brian very nearly missed being sent home at the end of his service. One day, after beach duty, the postman arrived and asked him why he was still there when other men he had arrived with had gone home two weeks earlier. Post haste he headed for the Orderly Officer, who told him that they were under the impression he was signing on as a regular. "It's been good, sir," said Brian "but not that good!" Two days later he was at Tripoli Airport, thankfully on his way home.

Edward Crook

Royal Engineers 1954-56

Edward was very nearly posted to Korea, where, although an armistice had been signed the previous year, a strong military presence was still required. But the posting was cancelled, and instead he was sent to a much more pleasant location: Tripoli.

Called up at 21 in 1954, after he had completed his apprenticeship as a plumber, Edward trained as a Motor Transport driver. The test was rigorous, and only one third of trainees passed. Edward was one, and the qualification covered driving three-ton trucks as well as Land Rovers and staff cars. Once in Libya, he was lucky enough to be selected as driver for the squadron's Officer Commanding (OC), Major McKenzie, whom Edward described as 'a real gent'. He remained his driver for the rest of his service.

One of the major's accomplishments was playing the bagpipes, and his oft-repeated instruction to Edward when preparing to go anywhere was "Don't forget the bagpipes!" He gave lessons to the Libyan Police Band, who, bizarrely, were very keen to learn the bagpipes!

Locusts were a major problem in Libya. Millions would descend on an agricultural area and totally destroy it, and one of the OC's jobs was to organise spotter planes to look for swarms and spread poison. Edward would drive him to meet up with the aircraft pilots to find out where the locusts were likely to attack.

One of the Major's interests was archaeology, and they would often visit Roman sites. Edward learned a great deal from these trips. Sometimes they went out into the desert on 'fitness for war' schemes. However, there was always a risk of getting lost in the vast featureless areas, and to avoid this happening they used sun compasses to help them find markers located around the area. These compasses had to be reset every hour.

On one occasion they met some Bedouin, and the Major engaged them in conversation. This resulted in an invitation to take tea, their hosts managing to entertain them in their limited English. For Edward this was an occasion he would always remember: sitting cross legged

The theatre at Leptis Magna; one of the many Roman sites in Libya

on a carpet outside a tent drinking black tea with a family of Bedouins!

Life in Libya for Edward was very pleasant. When not required for driving duties he was able to go to the nearby beaches and enjoy swimming in the warm Mediterranean water. He ended his National Service in 1956, fortunately just getting out before the Suez crisis.

Richard White

RAF 1955-57

Another National Serviceman who came very close to being involved in the Suez conflict was Richard White. He was on embarkation leave prior to being posted to Hong Kong when a telegram arrived ordering him to return his base at RAF Wharton, Lancs. He was told that he was going to Egypt, and was transported to Southampton. He assumed that he would be travelling by sea, but to his surprise he found himself boarding a Solent flying boat, a civilian version of the wartime Sunderland, and enjoyed a luxury flight at the expense of the RAF. After seven hours they landed at Malta, then boarded a Valetta for the onward journey to Libya. This was considerably less comfortable. The Valetta was a freight transport, and had no seats, so for this flight they had to sit on the floor! The reason for the flight was that his presence was urgently required in Libya in preparation for the Suez invasion, and the sea journey would have taken too long.

As a cadet in the Air Training Corps, Richard had learned some Morse, which was useful when he went into the RAF, where he spent six months training to transmit and receive messages in Morse, using the Marconi Adcock High Frequency transmitting system. He worked in Air Traffic Control at Barton Hall, near Preston, transmitting weather information and providing high frequency radio direction finding services, all in Morse. On one occasion he went on a NATO exercise in Malta, in an underground communication centre at RAF Lucca. He spent about five weeks there, enjoying the comfort of a hotel rather than barracks.

In Libya, Richard was based at RAF Castel Benito, near Tripoli. A very comfortable former Italian Air Force base, it was used at the time as a staging post for flights from the UK to the Middle East and was therefore of strategic importance in the Suez Conflict. Although in the end the fighting was very brief, he remained there for several months, enjoying the facilities of the base, which included a swimming pool.

As they were in a war zone, all mail was censored. Richard tried to circumvent this by writing home in Welsh, his first language. However, unbeknown to him, the chaplain was Welsh speaking and was able to translate his letters. Richard was reprimanded and told to write in English from then on!

Richard's return to the UK was also by air, this time in the comfort of a Comet of Transport Command.

Rolfe Mitchell

Royal Army Ordnance Corps 1950-52

Pyle is a small former mining town between Porthcawl and Port Talbot. Rolfe Mitchell was born and brought up there, and lives there still, but until he went into the Army he had rarely travelled far beyond its boundaries. People from Pyle did not go to exotic places when Rolfe was growing up, and when he found himself posted to North Africa he felt he was entering another world.

Rolfe was called up in May 1950, and after basic training at Aldershot he was posted to the Royal Army Ordnance Corps. This was the regiment that was responsible for the supply of weapons and equipment, and its role, though not glamorous, was to provide the vital support that enabled the fighting regiments to operate.

In September of that year Rolfe was posted to Tripoli, the capital of Libya. Although it had been under British control since liberation from Italy in 1943, the Italians still did the day-to-day running of the country, while the native Libyans were employed to do the menial labouring tasks. Rolfe worked alongside Italian civilians at first, and although fraternisation was officially discouraged, he found them warm and friendly colleagues.

Tripoli was at that time a beautiful city, very Italian in its atmosphere with elegant architecture and an abundance of cafes and restaurants, and it was here that Rolfe was first introduced to pasta. Unknown in Britain at the time, it has of course since become hugely popular. Many years later, Rolfe revisited the city, and was dismayed to find it now ugly and sprawling.

After three months in Tripoli Rolfe was moved to a mobile unit supplying small arms and motor spares to the 1st Infantry Division. Working from a caravan, his job was taking and processing orders. Meanwhile, in nearby Egypt, resentment at British occupation was building up and his unit was flown to the Canal Zone to reinforce the military presence there. Rolfe continued doing the same work, but life was considerably less comfortable. They now lived under canvas and slept on stretchers. Rolfe remained here until his discharge in May 1952.

Rolfe's two years in the Army taught him a great deal about life. He experienced the close comradeship of men from a variety of backgrounds who were thrown together for this period of their lives. Parting from them at the end of his service was, he said "like death". The boy who had left the village at eighteen came back a man of the world two years later, though not without some embarrassing experiences along the way.

In Malta, for example, where they spent a week en route to Libya, he and his mates decided to visit an infamous night spot known as The Gut. Having only enough to buy one beer each, they were surprised to find a not only a second drink brought with each pint, but women too, one for each of them!

To their horror, they realised that these were prostitutes, for whom they would be expected to buy the drinks, and no doubt much more. As one man they did the only thing possible – they fled!

A more poignant memory was of when they were on exercise in the desert. Rolfe was on guard duty on his own, pacing back and forth in the pitch dark, when he fell into an old slit trench, a leftover from the war, and rather than climb out he decided to stay there. Staring up at the night sky brilliant with stars, he felt homesick for the one and only time during his service.

Though Rolfe never came under enemy attack, life was not without its dramatic moments. One night, in the Canal Zone, he awoke to find armed guards everywhere. It seemed the NAAFI tent had accidentally caught fire, but as sabotage had been suspected there had been much commotion during the night. Rolfe, in his caravan, had slept through it all!

An important lesson he learned was to respect people of other races, something very lacking in the British Army at that time. One day he had what he calls 'a Damascene moment' (i.e. a revelation such as that experienced by Saint Paul on the road to Damascus). He and a group of other squaddies were watching a Libyan boy of about sixteen as he cleaned the barracks, and were making uncomplimentary remarks concerning his mother's sexual habits. The boy probably did not speak English but he clearly understood the implication of their words. Unable to retaliate for fear of instant dismissal, he turned on them a look that Rolfe has never forgotten. "It was a look of absolute pure hatred," he said. "It stopped me in my tracks. What would my father think, a man of high moral standards?" What he learned that day was that this boy and his race, whom the British arrogantly and disparagingly referred to as 'Wogs', were human beings just like him, with human feelings, and were entitled to be treated as such.

Rolfe completed his service with the rank of Corporal and a Canal Zone campaign medal (which he has never worn!). He was offered the rank of Sergeant if he chose to stay on in the Army, but he decided not to do so, and in May 1952 returned to his home in Pyle.

OTHER OVERSEAS POSTINGS

David Donne

REME 1952-54

Between 1950 and 1953 Britain had over 90,000 troops fighting in Korea, many of them National Servicemen. The country had been divided along the 38th Parallel in 1945 between Russian forces liberating the country from the Japanese in the north and Americans doing the same in the south, and the cause of the fighting was the attempt by soldiers of the North Korean Army, backed by Chinese troops, to take possession of the south.

The United Nations sent troops to the defence of the south. They were mainly American, but the British Government felt obliged to support them, even though it was stretched to the limits with other defence commitments. The fighting was fierce, and it developed into a war of attrition, like the First World War. Eventually an armistice was signed, which brought an end to the fighting, but a peace treaty was never signed, so that technically North and South Korea are still at war today, more than 65 years later. The 38th parallel remains the border between the two countries.

David Donne, from Skewen, near Port Talbot, had served in the Merchant Navy for two years before he was called up for National Service in 1952. After training in Colchester and Chatham he was posted with the Royal Electrical and Mechanical Engineers to Germany as a tank repair engineer. After a short time in Germany (where he visited the nearby Belsen Concentration Camp and was horrified by what he saw) he was sent on to Korea. There he spent the rest of his National Service, retrieving and repairing tanks that had been damaged in the conflict, which often placed him under enemy fire. He was lucky to escape injury when doing this and also when it was discovered that a dirt road along which he frequently travelled had an unexploded mine in the middle!

The weather conditions in Korea were appalling - unbearably hot in summer, freezing cold in winter. They lived twenty to a hut with a stove in the middle, on which a bowl of ice was placed in the mornings to provide water for all the men to wash in. It must have been fairly unpleasant by the time it was the last man's turn! They sometimes had to sleep outdoors in temperatures well below zero, keeping their rifles in their sleeping bags to prevent them from freezing up.

Few people back in Britain were aware of the dreadful conditions in Korea. David's mother sent copies of the local papers which claimed that "our boys are well looked after. They often have chicken to eat" but in reality they only got the wings while the officers had the breast. Their only luxury was a tin of peaches every Sunday. David became aware of the extreme poverty of the local people when the children came to collect the empty tins and flattened them to make tiles for their homes.

The British troops were also aware of the contrast between their conditions and those of the Americans, who were better fed, better paid, and better housed. Yet they sometimes came across to try to buy the British rifles. Whether they were better than the American models or the soldiers just wanted them for souvenirs is not known.

David Donne on active service in Korea

Needless to say, nobody was willing to sell his rifle for fear of court martial and a spell in a military prison.

Life was not without its occasional funny side. The latrine, an open pit in the ground, became unbearably smelly in the summer, and one day someone tossed a lighted match into it. The result was a mighty explosion. Hopefully nobody was standing too close to the fallout!

Korea was one of the worst postings for a National Serviceman, for here they encountered fighting conditions as bad as any in the Second World War, and they were not even defending their country. Small wonder that many came back bitter and resentful.

However, David was not put off army life. After demob he volunteered for the Territorial Army, was promoted to sergeant, and spent two weeks every year on training, usually in Germany. The advantage for him was that he was not only getting paid by the Army but also by his firm. It must also have been a relief not to be facing enemy fire.

Sadly, David has now passed away, and I am most grateful to his widow, Patricia, for supplying me with his story.

Basil Craddock MBE

Royal Military Police 1948-50

There cannot be many people in the world who can say that the ability to reassemble a dismantled bicycle pump changed their lives, but Basil Craddock is one of them!

Having done his basic National Service training, he applied to join the Military Police. The aptitude test was to put together a bicycle pump. Basil, a cycle owner whose pump frequently came apart, was so used to this operation that he could do it with his eyes shut, so within a couple of minutes the job was done and he was accepted into the Royal Military Police.

How this bizarre test demonstrated an aptitude for the work he was to do remains a mystery, but it changed his life because had he not gone into the Military Police he might never have then gone on to join the civilian police, and his life would have taken a totally different course.

Born the son of a miner in Bargoed, in the Rhymney Valley, Basil worked as a fireman on the Great Western Railway after leaving school and was called up on 30th May 1948. After two weeks of basic training with the Welch Regiment in Brecon, and having passed the bicycle pump test, he was posted to Inkerman Barracks, the headquarters of the RMP. It was a huge, draughty Victorian building in Woking, Surrey, formerly a women's prison and subsequently a mental hospital.

Life was hard. All soldiers were subjected to intense 'bull' during their training, but for an MP the standard was unbelievably high, and continued that way throughout their service. The 'Redcaps', as they were known throughout the army, had to be the very smartest, with snow white webbing belt and gaiters, highly polished brasses, knife-edge creases in their trousers, and boots like mirrors. Woe betide any man whose appearance was anything but immaculate, and many off-duty hours were spent applying Brasso, Blanco and boot polish.

Six months into his service, Basil was posted to Trieste, a port on the Adriatic. It lies on the Istrian Peninsula, an ethnically and culturally mixed area between Italy and Yugoslavia. At this time it was divided into two zones of occupation, one controlled by British and US forces, the other by Yugoslavia, which had a Communist government. The British contingent was BRETFOR, which stood for British Element Trieste Force. Trieste was an important entry point for allied troops and supplies for Austria, which had been under British occupation since the

Basil Craddock outside his home
in Bargoed

Inkerman Barracks, Surrey. Headquarters of The Royal Military Police

end of the war, so it was necessary to have a military garrison there to protect it from communist incursion.

The duties of the Military Police were mainly patrolling the streets from 7 pm until 1 am, keeping an eye on off-duty military personnel, making sure they were properly dressed and generally behaving themselves, especially keeping away from the brothels, which were out of bounds. Even such a seemingly trivial offence as having a button undone could result in the issue of a '252' form, which meant that the person had to report to his commanding officer for disciplinary action. Basil only once issued one of these, and afterwards regretted it, for a warning would have been sufficient. Heavy-handedness only served to make the 'Redcaps' even more unpopular.

Trieste was a pleasant posting. The conduct of the British troops was generally good, and Basil never had to break up any fights. The Italian people were extremely friendly, and the climate was benign.

Basil finished his service on 13th May 1950. For a time he returned to his old job as a railway fireman, but then tired, as he put it, "of coal dust under my fingernails" and, having enjoyed police work during his National Service, decided to join the Glamorgan Constabulary. He rose to the rank of Inspector, and after retirement became a County Court Bailiff. He was honoured for his services with the award of the MBE by the Queen.

Basil enjoyed his National Service. He liked the comradeship of the Army, the feeling of loyalty it engendered, and he felt it greatly broadened his outlook on life.

Geoff Mitchell

RAF 1957-59

Geoff's first posting in the RAF was almost down the road from his home; his second was to the other side of the world!

Having completed his eight weeks 'square bashing' at Bridgnorth, he went to RAF Kidbrook, in South East London, to be trained as a surface movements clerk, which involved organising the transportation of RAF personnel or goods by road, rail or sea. He spent an enjoyable three months wandering on and off ships in the incredible bustle of London Docks, checking RAF cargoes being loaded, and being based in Kidbrook gave him the great advantage of easily being able to get home to Shirley, near Croydon, at weekends.

However, when this work was taken over by a civilian firm, Geoff was posted to a totally different location: Goose Bay, in Canada. From the frantic bustle of the docklands, he now found himself in the remotest of places, where there was no road or railway at all and the only way in and out was by air and sea. The bay was frozen for nine months of the year, and only one ship arrived during his posting there.

Goose Bay was a stopping-off base for aircraft on their way to Christmas Island, where atomic weapons were being tested. It was jointly occupied by the Royal Canadian Air Force on one side and the United States Air Force on the other. Geoff was one of a small contingent of RAF personnel based on the Canadian side. Although it was possible

The Avro Vulcan was a jet-powered tailless delta wing high-altitude strategic bomber, operated by the RAF from 1956 until 1984. A total of 134 Vulcans were built, 45 to the B1 design, 89 as B2 models.

to go over to the US area, there was a limit as to how much they could spend there, so they stayed mainly on their own side.

Here Geoff spent a very pleasant year amongst a good group of mates. There was a cinema, swimming pool, badminton court, roller and ice skating rinks, where curling and ice hockey were also played. Through the availability of a record player, he developed an interest in classical music. They also had access to a television for a time, and there was a chess club. He retrained as an air movements clerk, organising the loading of aircraft and the feeding and accommodation of personnel passing through. At times it was busy, but there were also long quiet spells, so recreation facilities were much appreciated.

Geoff recalls one dramatic incident. As a Vulcan touched down, flames shot out of one of the wheels. Everyone grabbed a fire extinguisher and ran across to fight the fire, at considerable risk to themselves. By the time the airfield firefighters arrived, it had been put out. The cause was discovered to be a brake that had locked on one of the wheels, the consequent friction causing the flames. Another frightening incident occurred when Geoff was a passenger on a test flight in a Comet when the engines cut out in the cold air over Goose Bay. Thankfully the pilot managed to get them re-started and landed the aircraft safely.

Another time they were expecting a visit from the Queen, and all the stops were pulled out to make the base spick and span, but for reasons nobody could explain, Her Majesty never came!

Despite the very different postings, Geoff enjoyed his National Service. He felt it had given him self-confidence that he had lacked previously, and an opportunity to spend time in a very different part of the world.

Colin Davies

Royal Electrical and Mechanical Engineers 1958-60

As overseas postings go, Paris would be pretty high on any National Servicemen's wish-list, and it was to Supreme Headquarters Allied Powers Europe (SHAPE) at Voluceau, 5 kilometres east of Versailles, that Colin was sent to replace another National Servicemen who was coming to the end of his time. This was the headquarters of the North Atlantic Treaty Organisation (NATO) in Europe, and Colin spent 18 very comfortable months there.

Called up in January 1958, he was sent to do his basic training in Honiton, in a run-down camp where the hut roofs leaked and life was fairly unpleasant. Assigned to REME he did his training as a mechanic at Tewkesbury, although he had already completed a five-year apprenticeship, prompting his training officer to say "You're more qualified than I am!"

On standby for a posting to Yemen, he was asked if he would like to go to Paris. Yemen or Paris? It didn't take much thinking about, and in no time he was on the train to the Gare du Nord, where he and a sergeant bound for the same place were met by two American military policemen, who marched them to a big, shiny Chevrolet Bel Air. They were in no rush, and took them for a leisurely drive round Paris before going on to Valuceau. There Colin was amazed by the sumptuous luxury of this very modern establishment, with shops, cafeterias, a bowling alley and a dance floor. The rooms even boasted underfloor heating! A bus ran every 20 minutes into Paris, although civilian clothes had to be worn because of the danger of terrorist attack. Before long, Colin knew Paris like the back of his hand. On Sundays he attended the English Methodist Church, where he was warmly welcomed.

Colin's duties were to service and maintain all the motor vehicles on the camp, but he was also required to go on exercises from time to time. One of these was in a forest a few miles from Versailles. They were camped near a high wall, on the other side of which tank crews were training. At times they were coming very close to the wall, and Colin was worried that they might actually hit the wall and bring it crashing down! On another occasion they had to camouflage themselves and their vehicles, and their sudden noisy arrival at a site where a family had up till then been peacefully picnicking caused the terrified family to hastily grab their possessions and flee!

One of Colin's abiding memories was driving a 40 ton Scammell lorry down the Champs Elysee, which no doubt caused a few exclamations of "Sacrebleu!" among the astonished population.

Colin did not particularly want to do National Service, but he knew it would be difficult to find a job until he had done so, as employers were reluctant to take men on knowing that they would soon lose them for two years. Nevertheless he had 18 very pleasant months in Paris, so it could have been a lot worse!

Maldwyn Green

Royal Corps of Signals 1960-63

Worse fates could befall a National Serviceman than a four-month posting to the sunshine of the West Indies – a tough job, but someone had to do it! It was to British Guiana (now Guyana) that Maldwyn Green was flown as part of a contingent of British troops to restore order following an attempt to overthrow Prime Minister Cheddi Jagan in 1961. However, by the time they arrived the troubles were over, but the troops remained for the next four months just to make sure the situation remained stable. Maldwyn recalls this as a very pleasant time, during which he served as a batman to Major (later General) Hamish McKinley and other officers, a 'cushy' job which got him, among other privileges, excused from guard duties.

Maldwyn was among the last to be called up for National Service, and knowing that it was coming to an end did his best to try to avoid it. At his medical he claimed to suffer from migraine, reporting symptoms that he had looked up in the medical dictionary. He was sent home, apparently successful, but a month later he was sent to a consultant, who quickly saw through the fake symptoms and told him that two years in the army was the perfect cure for migraine!

He did his training at Catterick and became a teleprinter messenger in the Royal Corps of Signals, but was attached to the Coldstream Guards on Salisbury Plain. He was able to go home on the Silverline bus every weekend, but they had to be on 24 hour standby to be sent wherever they were needed. It was on one of these occasions that they were taken to Heathrow Airport and flown in a chartered aircraft to British Guiana to deal with the insurgency there. During the four months they spent there they lived very comfortably in commandeered civilian houses.

A keen sportsman, Maldwyn spent a lot of time playing tennis for the regiment, enjoying the privileges that the services always gave to those who were good at sport. However, army life had not always been pleasant. During basic training, which he describes as 'traumatic', he once dropped his rifle, and was screamed at by the corporal and called, bizarrely, a 'Welsh communist'!

Towards the end of his two years, Maldwyn was told that he would have to serve an extra six months, as not enough volunteers were being recruited to fill the gaps created by the ending of National Service. To many, this would have seemed an unacceptable imposition on top of the two years that had already been taken from their lives, but Maldwyn did not particularly mind. He was enjoying his time in the army, and for these last six months he would be paid as a regular – £3 a week, a considerable sum compared to the niggardly wages of a National

Serviceman. He spent these months in Germany, based in Dusseldorf. He even learned a little German – the only phrase a British soldier needed to learn: "Drei Bier, bitte"!

Herbert Martin

RAF 1945-48

Although he missed the war by just two months, Herbert was not immune to danger during his National Service in the RAF. Posted to Palestine when the British Army was desperately trying to curb the terrorist activities of the Zionists who were trying to establish a Jewish state in the face of bitter hostility by the Arabs, he had a lucky escape when a terrorist's bullet hit the wall just above his head. He did not even have the protection of a steel helmet. Another time he came under mortar fire and crawled under a vehicle. It stopped after four bombs had been launched, but he had felt extremely frightened while it was going on.

Herbert's first overseas posting was to Egypt, which involved a long overland journey to the South of France and then a sea crossing to Port Said. Trained as a driver, he was seconded to the Chaplaincy Branch, where his job was to chauffeur the padre in a fifteen hundredweight Dodge truck. Nearby was an encampment of German prisoners of war awaiting repatriation. Despite being battle-hardened Afrika Korps men, they were not guarded, nor did they make any attempt to escape. They were, however, armed with baseball bats, but that was to stop the locals from stealing from them! Herbert had regular contact with them, supplying a gramophone and records, which was much appreciated. He found them friendly and helpful, especially when he needed to solve problems with diesel engines, on which they were experts.

In July 1946 he was posted to Palestine, where he was assigned to be a driver for one of the principals of the RAF School of Moral Leadership, Wing Commander R R Clements. As part of this ten-day course he took the students in a Trooper truck fitted with seats to places of interest such as Bethlehem and the Old City in Jerusalem. He also did a half-day trip to the Dead Sea, where he recalls reading a book while floating on water so salty that it was impossible to sink! He was not pleased, however, that it took about two weeks to get the salt out of his hair! He drank water from Jacob's Well in Shechem, from which Jesus was said to have drunk, and visited the ruins of Tiberias, on the Sea of Galilee. To a young man with a religious upbringing this would all have been fascinating.

Even more thrilling was Christmas 1946, which he spent in - of all places - Bethlehem! He had driven three padres and their wives there, and they sang carols in the Fields of the Shepherds. For Herbert, it was an unforgettable experience.

When the Moral Leadership School closed, Herbert's main job became chauffeuring staff officers around the various bases in Palestine. It was hard driving over rough sandy roads, without the assistance of synchromesh gearboxes. In the two years he was overseas, he drove some 30,000 miles.

British soldiers in Palestine had the difficult and unenviable task of

The Church of the Nativity, in Bethlehem. Its grotto holds a prominent religious significance to Christians as the birthplace of Jesus.

trying to keep the peace between Arabs and Jews. On one occasion Herbert witnessed an assassination attempt on an Arab who had tried to sell land to a Jew. He had to attend an identity parade, but refused to pick out a suspect, not only for fear of reprisal but because he did not want to condemn a man to death. Another time he was just minutes away from the explosion of a petrol tanker to which a limpet mine had been attached. This was his third near-death experience.

After twelve months (extended from six) in Palestine, Herbert went back to Egypt and thence to Aden, which, with its black sandy soil, he found a very inhospitable place. He was there until April 1948, when his service in the RAF ended. Like Llew Williams (q.v.) he began his National Service just after the end of the war, before it was fixed at two years, and served for a total of three.

Home Postings

SOME MEN WOULD like to have been posted overseas but were not offered the possibility, usually because their services were required in the UK. Others chose a home posting so as not to be too far from their families in case of emergency. While some home postings may have seemed disappointing, they could still offer interesting and varied experiences.

John Pearman

King's Own Royal Regiment 1956-58

January 1958 was one of the coldest months on record, and arguably the worst place to be at that time was the Brecon Beacons, but that was where Second Lieutenant John Pearman and his platoon found themselves one bitter night. His orders were to dig in and prepare for a possible attack, but the soil was rock hard and digging to any depth impossible. They did the best they could, and waited. All night they waited, until by six am, perished with cold, they decided there was not going to be an attack and they could have breakfast. Then, just as they were enjoying a hot and very welcome meal, the attack came and they were totally unprepared. It was

a hard lesson of warfare learned that morning... always expect the unexpected!

As a young officer, John was aware of the awesome responsibility of leadership. A wrong decision on his part could have cost the lives of the platoon of men that he was leading one night towards an isolated farmhouse. In the pitch darkness, he was not even sure he was going in the right direction, but suddenly, and to his immense relief, the moon came out and there, in the distance, stood the farmhouse. His accurate navigation earned him a 'well done' from his Commanding Officer.

This was only an exercise, but it brought home to John the value of meticulous planning that he had been taught during his officer training. Had this been a real war zone, any lack of competence on his part could have resulted in the death of the men under his command. It was, he said, good preparation for the decision making he would have to make in his working life in the steel industry.

John was called up in September 1956. He was well prepared for military life, having been a member of the Combined Cadet Force at boarding school in Monmouth, and, being accustomed to life away from home, he did not suffer the homesickness that afflicted many a new recruit.

John Pearman, left, on exercise on the Brecon Beacons

Basic training was at Dorchester Barracks for two weeks, followed by ten weeks at Topsham Barracks in Exeter. One of his memories of that time was standing by the barbed wire fence surrounding the camp and feeling, as he watched people on the other side going about their normal lives, as though he had lost his freedom, and for the next two years he would be the property of the Army.

John was selected for officer training. Normally, this took two years, but for National Servicemen it was reduced to just four months. It took place at Eaton Hall, in Chester, and was extremely intensive. On completion, he was commissioned in the King's Own Royal Regiment, based in Lancaster. Exercises were held on the North York Moors, another hostile and challenging environment. Here they trained as infantry units of the Lightning Brigade, ready to go anywhere at short notice, and were at one stage about to be deployed to Kuwait, but were stood down at the last minute.

However, not all John's challenges were on the battlefield. He wrote "I vividly recall the occasion of the platoon's imminent departure to Kuwait when my Commanding Officer told me to talk to the young soldiers on the importance of keeping away from 'unsociable places' and avoiding venereal disease. At a total loss as to how to even begin to carry out the CO's instruction, I was spared further embarrassment when, to my relief, my captain told me to go and check out the armoury and weapon requirements while he gave the talk to the men!"

No such lack of confidence was evident in the behaviour of John and his fellow officer cadets when seeking to introduce themselves to a group of attractive young ladies travelling home from college for the Christmas holiday. "Finding ourselves on the same train from Chester Station, we young officers, confident in trench coats and peaked caps, called on the army's tactical weapon of surprise by inviting the students to join us for a cup of tea! As a result, I have now been married to my wonderful wife Gillian for 57 years, the outcome of a successful military mission!"

John very much enjoyed his time in the Army, and was sorry to leave in September 1958. He might have stayed on had he not got a place at Cambridge University to read history. It took him the best part of a year to settle to the very different life of an undergraduate, with its requirement for academic discipline gradually evolving out of the essentially physical and rigorous pattern of his valued army service.

He still keeps in contact with his old regiment.

Mike Mansley

RAF 1950-52

Of the many who did their National Service in the RAF, Mike was the only one of my interviewees who actually flew on active service. During his first week or so of training, he and his fellow recruits were marched to the Astra Cinema at RAF Padgate to watch a film about opportunities to train for aircrew. This offered not only the excitement of flying, but an increase in pay, and promotion to either sergeant or officer. Having the necessary School Certificate, and being adjudged medically fit, Mike was sent with his fellow would-be aircrew to RAF Hornchurch, in Essex, to attend a selection board. He passed, and was assigned to train as an Aircrew Signaller, which suited him as he had learned Morse in his school cadet corps.

At that time, RAF Coastal Command was expanding to meet the threat posed by a build-up of Russia's submarine fleet during the Korean War, and was happy to include National Servicemen to fulfil its manpower requirement. The initial training for Mike's new role lasted for several months, and it was not until August 1951 that he first boarded an Avro Anson, with five other trainees, at RAF Swanton Morley, near Norwich. They were required to use their Morse keys, radio transmitters and receivers to communicate with HQ. The flight almost ended in disaster - one of the wheels refused to descend as they came in to land, and the sight of ambulances and fire engines on standby on the runway caused some extremely anxious moments. Fortunately, after strenuous efforts by the crew, the wheel did come down and they landed safely.

On one occasion, Mike was preparing to board a two-seater Percival Proctor with a Polish Battle of Britain veteran at the controls. His English was limited, and when he said "Tail!" it took Mike some time to realise that he was required to sit on the tail of the aircraft while the pilot taxied to the take-off point, to prevent the aircraft turning over in the strong wind. Mike spent many anxious moments as the speed of the propeller gradually increased, hoping that his laconic pilot had not forgotten about him! Fortunately, he had not.

Mike Mansley, in doorway, boarding a Shackleton

By February 1952 he was adjudged to be competent to join an operational training unit and was sent to RAF St Mawgan, in Cornwall, a Maritime Reconnaissance School where crews were trained to hunt and destroy enemy submarines. The aircraft in which they flew was the Lancaster, which had played a pivotal role in Bomber Command a few years earlier. By the end of his training, Mike had flown a grand total of 97 hours.

In June 1952 he was sent to RAF Kinloss, in the north of Scotland, where he trained to fly in the Shackleton, the successor to the now obsolete Lancaster. Here they carried out radar guided bombing exercises and gunnery tests. On one occasion they were forced to make an emergency landing when three of the four engines died!

After some 68 hours of flying at Kinloss, Mike was judged to be fit to join an operational unit and was posted to join 240 Squadron at RAF Ballykelly, in Northern Ireland. Though it was peacetime, he received a chilling reminder of the dangers of flying when he was allocated his quarters. On entering the hut, he found the wardrobes full of clothes. They belonged to two men who had recently died when their Shackleton had crashed into the North Sea during an exercise. Unfortunately nobody had remembered to remove their possessions before Mike had arrived.

Their first flight from Ballykelly was an 18 hour trip that took them over Iceland to Jan Mayen Island, where they were treated to the spectacle of the Land of the Midnight Sun. The long flight was made relatively comfortable by the presence of an on-board grill and an engineer who was a good cook. There was also a bunk where they could relax when off duty.

Mike flew a total of 85 hours from Ballykelly, which included participation in a NATO exercise. For this they flew to Sola, a military station near Stavangar, in Norway. A former wartime Luftwaffe airfield, its accommodation was so spartan that a Canadian crew who were participating in the exercise refused to stay there and booked into a nearby hotel.

They were invited to a dance at the local community hall, and were looking forward to meeting blond young Norwegian ladies. Sadly, however, they found themselves surrounded by blond young Norwegian men, all eager to practise their English while the girls were kept elsewhere. They told their guests that during the German occupation, only boys had been taught English at school, so the girls were not able to join in the conversation. However, it was suspected that this was a ruse by the boys to ensure that the visitors were kept away from their girlfriends! Nevertheless, the visitors were impressed by the warmth of their reception by the Norwegians.

Mike's service in the RAF ended in October 1952, and although he was invited to sign on as a regular, he did not relish the prospect of a further eight years tapping out Morse messages, although he did spend some time in the RAF Reserve.

He had been only too pleased to be called up, as it enabled him to escape from a boring and repetitive job as a Civil Servant. However, in subsequent years he would gain far greater job satisfaction in the Royal Mint in London and Wales than would have been the case had he signed on in the RAF.

Geoff Davies

Royal Artillery 1952-54

Geoff's National Service was unusual in two respects. Firstly, although he was called up into the Royal Artillery, he served most of his time with the RAF; secondly, during this time he worked in a most unusual location: deep underground in a top secret nuclear bunker.

Geoff Davies, from Pontypridd, was called up in November 1952 and did his basic training at Oswestry. He recalls that it was bitterly cold in the barracks due to the constant failure of the central heating system. Water for washing and shaving was ice cold, and to keep warm in bed it was necessary to pile as much as possible on top of themselves: greatcoats, newspapers if available, and anything else that would provide a little extra insulation.

He also recalls the kit inspections, which would often take place shortly before 10 pm. Every man would be standing by his bed, his kit immaculately laid out, but should the eagle-eyed NCOs spot the slightest irregularity, they were likely to throw the offending items out of the window! The lights would then go out and the hapless offenders had to frantically search for their discarded belongings outside in the dark. It was a powerful incentive to get it right!

Ten weeks of purgatory at Oswestry was followed by six weeks clerical training at Woolwich Barracks. During this time London was flooded and the troops were called upon to help. Geoff was provided with a pair of waders which, unfortunately, were three sizes too small. No replacements were available, so he had to endure pinched feet until the floods subsided. He recalls arriving at the mess late one evening to discover that all the food had gone, and his meal consisted of ten pieces of Swiss Roll!

He was then posted to a small anti-aircraft battery at RAF Felixtowe, where he was pleased to discover that there was considerably less 'bull' in the Air Force than in the Army. There were very few parades or guard duties, and he no longer had to wear his belt and gaiters. In fact they became so unfamiliar to him that when he had to wear them for the train journey to the demob centre, he suddenly became aware, as he looked down, that his gaiters were on the wrong way round!

The AA unit was moved to RAF North Weald (a former Battle of Britain fighter station), in Essex. Its function there was to operate in conjunction with the plotters who controlled the movements of the aircraft, and its location was the lowest floor of Kelvedon Hatch Underground Bunker.

In the early 1950s, once Russia had become a potentially hostile nuclear power, the Government decided to build secret underground bunkers from which it could continue to operate in the event of a nuclear war. One of these was Kelvedon Hatch. Built in 1952-3, it was 125 feet deep on three floors, and protected by 400 tons of concrete.

It could accommodate around 500 personnel, with dormitories, catering facilities and a sick bay. It had central heating, air conditioning and a water supply, and was packed with the latest electronic communications equipment. Entry was through an innocuous-looking bungalow surrounded by woods.

It was maintained by the Ministry of Defence until 1992, when it was decommissioned following the end of the Cold War. It is now open to the public as a tourist attraction.

Kelveden Hatch 'Bungalow', set in woodland in Brentwood. It looks like a normal bungalow from the outside, but held many secrets within.

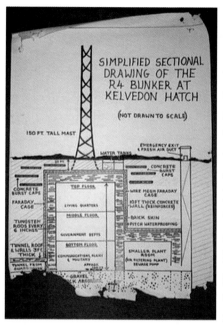

SIMPLIFIED SECTIONAL DRAWING OF THE R4 BUNKER AT KELVEDON HATCH
(NOT DRAWN TO SCALE)

This was where Geoff was to spend the rest of his National Service. Although he continued to wear Army uniform, he was, in effect, in the RAF, and would spend all his time, on or off duty, with airmen. He worked as a clerk to the Lieutenant Colonel in charge of the AA battery, though he admits that he never learned to type properly. He thought of applying for an overseas posting, but at that time could only have gone to Germany, which did not appeal to him, though he later regretted this decision.

Geoff had little difficulty in adapting to service life. Having been a boarder at Cowbridge Grammar School, he was used to communal living and bad food! He had spent his summer holidays at his grandfather's farm near Aberystwyth, so he was accustomed to being away from home. Overall, he enjoyed his National Service and had no problem making the transition back to civilian life. He returned to his former employment in Lloyds Bank, where he remained for the rest of his working life. He now lives in Porthcawl.

Graham Watkins

RAF 1956-58

Graham very quickly learned that musical ability was a considerable asset to a National Serviceman. He had just arrived at RAF Wilmslow to do his 'square bashing', and on the first muster parade came the call "All those who can play a musical instrument, step forward!" Ignoring, or possibly still unaware of, the serviceman's maxim, "Never volunteer

Graham Watkins in the office at RAF Valley

for anything", Graham did so, for not only could he play the piano and the violin, but he had also had some lessons on the clarinet at school. "So it was," he wrote, "that while the rest of the flight were on rifle drill or clumping around the parade ground in the cold autumn winds, I was in the comfort of the band room learning to play the various marches needed. Fortunately, next to me was an accomplished clarinet-tist who was able to show me the fingering of the notes I didn't know." The only military requirement during this time was a weekly training session with the RAF Regiment on the Bren gun. By the end of this period he reckoned he was able to strip and reassemble the weapon in the dark if necessary and was a sufficiently accurate shot to have won his marksmanship badge, though he cannot now remember if it was with the Bren or a .303 rifle.

Graham recalls with amusement the occasion when the band was playing for a passing-out parade of airmen and WAAFs. One of the buildings backing onto the parade ground was the shower block, the occupants of which, hearing the music, came up to the frosted glass windows to peer out of the openings at the top in order to see what was happening, unaware that their naked bodies were clearly visible to all, including the highly amused WAAFs! Order was restored when someone was hastily dispatched to the shower room to shoo them away from the windows.

Basic training (such as it was!) over, Graham applied to become a typist, in order to keep his fingers nimble, as he intended to pursue a career in music, and had a teacher training college place awaiting him when he finished his National Service. The centre for clerical training was RAF Creden Hill, near Hereford, and as his hand-eye co-ordination was already well established through playing the piano he found learning to type relatively easy. He continued his music as a member of the Station Band.

On completion of the course he requested a posting to a station in Wales, in the hope that he might be sent to RAF St Athan, which was just down the road from his home in Barry. This would have enabled him to work for his LRAM (Licentiate of the Royal Academy of Music) exam on the piano, having completed all the necessary previous exams. His hopes were dashed, however, when he learned that he was indeed to be posted to Wales, but to RAF Valley, in Anglesey, at the other end of the country! So much for his hopes of getting his 'letters'! The compensation, however, was an office with a spectacular view of Snowdon.

Valley was a flying station housing No 7 Flying Training School. Inevitably, there were crashes from time to time, and on the desk which Graham was allocated in the Station Sick Quarters was the 'crash phone'. When it rang, he had to answer it, take a map reference, and place a pin in the map of North Wales behind his desk. He then had to press two alarm buttons, one to alert the duty orderly driver, the other the duty medical officer. They would dash in, note the position of the pin and drive off at top speed in the ambulance. Like one of Pavlov's dogs, Graham was so conditioned to respond immediately to the sound of the crash bell that on one occasion, after he had left the RAF, hearing a similar sounding bell while sitting in a bench on Cardiff Station, he automatically leapt to his feet!

It was a comfortable posting. Accommodation was in well-built two storey blocks with mainly individual bedrooms. Graham was moved from the crash phone desk to one in the medical store with the view of Snowdon. As a trained typist he was much appreciated for the speed with which he was able to get the medical records up to date, to the relief of the struggling one-finger typists, and he set up a filing system for the Medical Officer's correspondence. The civilian cook in the sick quarters was a Mr Jones (one of several of that name on the camp, unsurprisingly!), who had been a chef on liners and produced tender steaks the like of which Graham had never before tasted. Thanks to Mr Jones, Graham left the Air Force no longer weighing just over seven stone with his ribs showing.

Valley was also the home of No 22 Search and Rescue helicopter squadron, (one of whose more recent pilots was HRH Prince William). Graham was surprised one Saturday morning, a time when flying practice did not normally take place, to hear the roar of a helicopter hovering outside. From the window he could see it at ground level with someone jumping out, bending over to pick something off the ground, then jumping back in again. "What on earth are they doing?" enquired Graham of one of the old hands. "Picking mushrooms for breakfast." came the reply. It was certainly a novel way of getting in one's flying hours! Likewise, a bottle of methylated spirit requested by 22 Squadron for their stove was collected by helicopter, despite the medical centre being only a short walk away.

Graham was able to continue practising music at Valley. Knowing that he intended to become a music teacher, his colleagues in the accommodation block were determined to ensure he absorbed as wide a range of music as possible, including big band, traditional jazz, modern jazz, and so on. "As long as the quality was good, I soon learned to appreciate the wide range of music. Beside playing in the forty-strong Station Band, I also played in the Sky Rockets. our dance band, not only for dances on camp but on other parts of Anglesey and the surrounding mainland Great fun, and a means of earning a penny or two!"

One of Graham's responsibilities was to keep the Queen's Regulations and Station Standing Orders files up to date, and this work led him to discover information about which the RAF had been keeping very quiet. One concerned payment for playing at church services, something which Graham had been doing for the Presbyterian, Methodist and United Board church twice a week for some time. The regulation stated that payment was to be made out of Air Force funds, and as Graham had kept a diary of all his services, he was able to make a list, which was signed by the padre and attached to his request for payment. Consequently, he received a substantial amount of back pay, sufficient to buy himself a decent raincoat. He also discovered that bandsmen were entitled to a second 'best blue' uniform instead of the usual battledress, at no cost to themselves, a privilege which he was quick to take advantage of.

As was usual in the RAF, 'bull' was kept to a minimum once basic training was over. Graham and his fellow occupants kept their quarters clean and tidy on a rota basis, two of them acting as duty orderlies every morning. An NCO would make an inspection and there was rarely a problem, until one day an officious RAF Regiment Sergeant, a long-term regular, was placed in charge. He began to make unnecessary and unreasonable demands, such as insisting that the gloss painted walls were washed down every morning. This caused great resentment, and often made the orderlies late for work.

However, the sergeant was up against men who may have been lower in rank but considerably smarter when it came to making life difficult. His allowance of coal somehow failed to be delivered to his married quarters; his pay was suddenly short because his allowances had been mysteriously omitted; his medical injections were discovered to be out of date, a situation which had to be immediately rectified. Questions were being asked higher up the chain of command as to why the billet orderlies were arriving late for work, and before long the unpopular sergeant found himself posted elsewhere, to everyone's relief, and life in the barracks returned to normal.

Graham even managed to get some flying in during his two years - a trip in an Anson to the Farnborough Air Show and a lift to South Wales in a Dragonfly helicopter.

Graham enjoyed his National Service. "The two years seemed to pass quickly. As an only child I felt my National Service was a useful ladder in growing up. I was pleased to have new skills at my fingertips, skills which were of great value to me in my profession and continue to be so."

Graham was kind enough to write an account for me of his RAF service, from which I have quoted in this piece.

Len Smith

Royal Army Medical Corps 1958-60

Len's National Service was considerably less arduous than that of many of his contemporaries. Firstly, it was not really an interruption to his career, because he continued to work as a pharmacist, a profession for which he had qualified before he was called up. Secondly, he was not posted overseas, where he might have faced a hostile enemy, but spent much of his time in the elegant surroundings of Sandhurst Military Academy. Finally, he enjoyed the additional privilege of having his new young wife with him for part of the time. Life could have been a lot worse!

Len spent two years after leaving school as an apprentice pharmacist with Boots in Risca, near Newport, and then went on to study at Cardiff University for a degree in pharmacy. He deferred his National Service until he had graduated, and was 25 when he was called up. A year earlier, in July 1957, he had married his fiancée, Primrose Earl, whom he had met while working at Boots.

Posted to Cookham Barracks, near Aldershot, Len did his basic training, which included First Aid and nursing. This normally lasted for eight weeks, but Len managed to miss the last two weeks by going to the Army School of Dispensing at Mytchett, in Surrey, to sit an exam in forensic pharmacy.

He was then posted to The Cambridge Hospital in Aldershot, a large military hospital catering for all the forces in the area, where he worked as a dispenser. He describes it as "a great experience. I learned how to produce medication in large amounts. We mixed our creams and ointments in a Kenwood food mixer. As army dispensers we did ward

Len Smith,
pictured in
RAMC
Number 1 Dress

rounds with the medical officers. Whilst on call one night I was asked to deliver some oxygen cylinders to the maternity ward. I had to gown up and connect the oxygen in the theatre. Whilst there I was invited to stay and witness the delivery of twins by Caesarean Section!"

Len's next posting was to the prestigious Royal Military Academy at Sandhurst to fill a vacancy created by the departure of a sergeant dispenser. Len was still only a private, and in the back of a military ambulance on its daily run to Sandhurst he had to change into a tunic on which he had sewn three stripes so that he would arrive as a sergeant.

The RMA had a 24 bed hospital which catered for the officer cadets and staff as well as their wives and children. Len's main role was to run the dispensary, but on one night in three he acted as wardmaster for the hospital. As the matron and sister were off duty, he was virtually in sole charge!

In addition to their normal hospital duties, the medical staff also had to provide cover for special events such as the passing-out parade, the army point-to-point horse racing at nearby Tweseldown, and for accidents which occasionally occurred on the training range.

The highlight of the year at Sandhurst is The Sovereign's Parade, which marks the passing out of the officer cadets at the end of their training, and is attended by VIPs, families and friends. Many hours of rehearsal go into this prestigious event, but unforeseen accidents can still happen. Len describes what occurred during a practice when he was on medical cover. "It was the last parade for the adjutant, who was retiring from the army, so the Regimental Sergeant Major called the parade to give him three cheers.

The procedure in the army is to raise your cap with the left hand above your head and return it smartly with the upper arm parallel with the ground. What had been forgotten was that the cadets all had fixed bayonets, and many of them brought their arms down on the bayonets of the cadets next to them! We had a busy day stitching up cuts, but the cadets were more upset that they had damaged their 'best blues' that they were to wear next day at the Sovereign's Parade."

Although Len held the rank of sergeant, his pay was considerably less than that of regular NCOs. His salary after a small allowance to his wife was £4.10s (£4.50 in today's money), whereas regular sergeants were receiving £23 to £35, depending on length of service. He could rarely afford to dine or drink in the Sergeants' Mess, so he normally ate in the hospital kitchen and socialised with the staff, usually playing cards. On one of the rare occasions that Len did go to the Sergeants' Mess he unwittingly incurred the wrath of the legendary Regimental Sergeant Major Lord, who boomed "Before you buy a beer you say Good Morning to me!"

Len had become friendly with a regular corporal clerk at the hospital called John, who with his wife Mary lived in married quarters in nearby Camberley. Knowing that Len was married, they kindly invited Prim to come and stay with them for a few weeks, which she was naturally very happy to do.

Len obtained a sleeping out pass, and only slept in the Academy when he was on call at night. Prim was pregnant at the time, and shortly after the visit their first son, Vaughn, was born. She made a second visit with Vaughn to look after Mary, who was pregnant after several miscarriages and managed to be successfully delivered of a healthy boy.

Len was demobbed in September 1960. He has a permanent reminder of his time at Sandhurst in the form of an inscribed pewter tankard from his colleagues in the Sergeants' Mess.

Les kindly lent me an account of his Service, from which I have quoted.

Howell Davies

Royal Artillery 1952-54

Howell was another of those fortunate men who was able to continue his peacetime trade during National Service. After just two weeks' basic training at Oswestry it was discovered that he had completed a five year apprenticeship as a signwriter, so he was called upon by one of the officers to be the Regimental Signwriter. Regiments were very proud of their insignia, and the ability to create signage that reflected this pride was a highly valued skill.

Howell's trade had guaranteed him a very comfortable National Service. From that point on he did no drill, no guard duties, no weapons training. One sergeant major tried to put him on a duty list but was overruled by the Commanding Officer. Clearly, Howell's time was too valuable to be spent on military duties! When his name appeared on a list for transfer to the Tank Corps, his CO said "You don't want to go to the Tank Corps, do you, Davies?" "No, sir" came the immediate reply, and Howell's name disappeared from the list. So in his own workshop in the corner of the Royal Electrical and Mechanical Engineers (REME) hut in Pembroke Dock, he spent his days making signs. When he was not engaged in Army work he was allowed to earn a bit of extra cash doing work for local shops.

However, there were times when he was called upon to do somewhat unorthodox jobs for an officer known as the Mad Major, so called because he had a habit of making the 'naughty boys' (i.e. soldiers who were on a charge) run across the field while he threw javelins at them, fortunately always missing! When he summoned Howell to his house (in a lorry that was always laid on) it was to do such non-military jobs as looking after his dogs while he went shopping, painting a door or doing a spot of wallpapering. It is unlikely that Howard had expected to be doing jobs like these during his National Service!

Howell spent some of his off-duty time practising athletics. He was a very good sprinter. Never a drinker, he did not spend time in the bar, preferring in his off-duty hours to enjoy his hobby of drawing and painting. Among his memories were seeing the Queen just after the

Coronation in 1953, and getting to see the final rehearsal for the Royal Tournament.

After demob, Howard resumed his trade, having had very little military experience during his two years!

Maldwyn Davies

RAF 1956-59

Sport was enthusiastically encouraged in the forces as a boost to morale, and those who were good at it were at a definite advantage, for they were excused many tedious duties so that they could devote their time and energy to sport, and could even enjoy the privilege of a special diet! Maldwyn's football skills were soon spotted and before long he became captain of the station team at RAF Innsworth, near Gloucester, where he was posted after basic training at Padgate. He also played for Home Command, which was of a high enough level to include professionals such as Tony Kay, who later played for Sheffield Wednesday. There was a down side, however. Maldwyn would like to have been posted abroad, but Warrant Officer Joe Blackwell, who was i/c football, blocked his application. He was too valuable to the team to be sent overseas!

Maldwyn was also able to get home most weekends to play for Kenfig Hill, his local team. On Sunday nights he would go to the cinema with his girlfriend but always had to leave before the film ended to catch his train back to Innsworth, and his early departures would often be marked with embarrassingly loud farewell greetings by his friends in the audience!

When he was called up, Maldwyn decided to sign on for three years. This meant not only that he was better paid but he was also had a choice of service and trade. So he went into the RAF accountancy branch, where he administered airmen's pay. He also studied for GCE O Level English, which he had missed at school due to illness. As he was the only member of the class, it was not really surprising that he passed!

He also passed his driving test while in the RAF, which saved him the expense of lessons.

When he was off duty, Maldwyn and his friends would go into Cheltenham, where there were dances organised by the personnel of a nearby American base. On return to camp they were not normally required to show their identity cards, as they were well known to the military police. One night, however, he was dismayed to discover an unusual number of policemen at the gate and he realised he did not have his ID card with him! So to avoid the possibility of a charge he decided to run round the perimeter to a place where he knew there was a gap in the fence. However, he was spotted by the police, who went in hot pursuit of him. He managed to get back to his billet, and leapt into bed fully clothed! He pulled the blankets over him and pretended to be asleep, and to his relief he was not discovered. The next morning everyone had to report to the main square for a parade. There they were informed that a woman had been raped the night before by a serviceman. Maldwyn, seen running off, had been pursued as a likely suspect!

He did get into potentially serious trouble on one occasion, however. In his office was a corporal who constantly taunted him, and this became unbearable one morning when Maldwyn had just received a 'Dear John' letter from his girlfriend, and was in a particularly angry mood. He could take no more of the corporal's sarcasm, and lashed out at him. Striking an NCO was a very serious offence, which could have resulted in a court martial, but the Commanding Officer, aware of the corporal's taunting, was sympathetic and sentenced Maldwyn to ten days CB (Confined to Barracks). An irksome punishment, but infinitely better than a spell in a military prison.

One weekend he and some others went to London, where they visited an establishment known as the Heaven and Hell Club, presided over by an enormous and powerful landlady who stood no nonsense from her guests. She would pick up men who were misbehaving by the scruff of the neck and the seat of their pants and bodily throw them out. Maldwyn's behaviour on that occasion caused him to be ejected in this unceremonious way!

One of his unsuccessful posting requests was to the Woomera Rocket

Range in Australia. This, like his others, was blocked by Warrant Officer Blackwell, but he later had cause to be grateful when he learned that it was located 200 miles from the nearest town, which only had about six houses and a pub.

One person who remains fixed in Maldwyn's memory was the female dentist in whose ample bosom the patients willingly rested their heads during treatment!

Although he missed out on the chance to go overseas, Maldwyn enjoyed his National Service. If nothing else, it gave him plenty of opportunities to develop his talent for sport.

Clive Edwards

RAF 1955-58

Clive's National Service did not get off to a good start. After just four days kitting out at Cardington (where he had been impressed by the gigantic former airship hangars) he was summoned home to attend court in connection with a minor traffic accident in his home village of North Cornelly, near Porthcawl. By the time he returned the rest of the group had moved on to Padgate for 'square bashing'. He made his way there to re-join them, but found himself immediately on 'jankers' for casually sauntering into the camp instead of marching!

However, things got better. He was assigned to a hut under the command of a corporal. Being skilled at calligraphy, he wrote his name on his locker card in script. Seeing this, the corporal asked who had done it, and when Clive said he had, asked him if he would do one for every locker in the hut, as this would help to win the cup for the best presented flight. Clive had already learned that in the forces you do not say no to a request from someone in authority, and did as he was asked. The flight sergeant then asked him to do a card for every locker in the flight. When Clive pointed out that he would not have time, he was told that he would be excused training so that he could spend all day at it if necessary. Sensing his advantage, he said he needed warm hands for the job, and was told that he could light the stove, normally forbidden during the daytime. Consequently, when the others came in at the end of a cold day on the parade ground, they were delighted to be greeted by the warmth in the hut, and Clive became very popular! In all, he managed to miss four weeks of training, but was still selected as marker on his passing out parade.

He was then posted to No 5 Personnel Despatch Unit at RAF Innsworth, near Gloucester, where he did the clerical work involved in moving people from training to posting to various commands around the UK. Rising through junior ranks, he was promoted to corporal within fifteen months. Every quarter, officers would arrive pleading for personnel, and he would have to try to meet their needs. He alternated this work with doing clerical statistics for two weeks, then returning to release from training for two weeks. Almost every other weekend he was able to get home. During the Suez crisis, however, it was a different situation. Clive and most others, except civilian staff, had to work round the clock to meet the demands of essential manpower movement to support this massive overseas operation.

Clive had the opportunity of postings to New York and Fontainbleu, but he did not have sufficient time left. He was glad he had rejected a posting to Christmas Island in view of the disastrous effect on the health of the men who had gone there to witness the testing of Britain's hydrogen bombs.

He enjoyed sport. Like Maldwyn Davies (qv), he played for RAF Innsworth's football team, which included Tony Kay, who went on to join Sheffield Wednesday, and Alan Williams (Bristol City). Also billeted close by was Tony Lewis, who subsequently played cricket for Glamorgan and rugby for Gloucester, captained the England cricket team and later became a sports writer and President of the MCC. Not that Clive saw a great deal of them, for like all talented sportsmen they were given generous amounts of time off to train and play.

Clive had signed on for three years to ensure he got into the RAF, had enjoyed the benefits of being a regular, had played a lot of sport and considered extending his term, but in the end decided to return to civilian life.

Alan Ward

RAF 1959-61

The Queen's Colour Squadron of the RAF has for many years delighted audiences at events such as the Royal Tournament with exhibition drill displays, in which for twenty minutes a complex sequence of moves is carried out without a single word of command being given. The QCS also provides a ceremonial guard to visiting dignitaries and represents the RAF at events such as the annual Festival of Remembrance. It was manned largely by National Servicemen (mainly because they had recently spent a lot of time on the drill square) until it was taken over by the RAF Regiment, and it was in this prestigious unit that Alan Ward spent a large part of his National Service.

"They didn't really want us," said Alan, who began his service in March 1959, a year before the last National Servicemen were called up. The service chiefs were now planning for long term enlistments, but still had to find something to occupy their final conscripts for two years.

Although he came close to being called up at 18 because of the Suez Crisis, Alan managed to complete his apprenticeship as a draughtsman before he went into the RAF at 21. He spent his first eight weeks on basic training at Bridgnorth, during which he was sometimes ordered to perform idiotic tasks such as cutting the grass with scissors!

His training completed, Alan was offered two options: work in the cookhouse or become a drill instructor. Not keen on spending his days peeling potatoes, he opted for the latter. That took up eight weeks, but after that his services were not required, so again he was offered two choices: the cookhouse or the Queen's Colour Squadron. It took no thinking about, and for the next fifteen months he was based at RAF Uxbridge, in London, the home of the QCS, from which he toured the country as part of the drill display team. Their duties also included mounting guard for the Queen on ceremonial occasions, lining the route for the wedding of Princess Margaret, for the Lord Mayor's Show, and for visiting VIPs such as General de Gaulle and King Hussein of Jordan.

However, Alan's time was not taken up entirely with ceremonial duties. At Uxbridge he worked with the Education Officer, helping

Queen's Colour Squadron of the RAF marching from St James's Palace to the changing of the Guard (Dirk Ingo Franke at www.wikipedia.org)

airmen to improve their basic maths and reading skills. He also had to take his turn with guard duties, though he was given time off afterwards, and over his two years in the RAF he clocked up a total of 187 days' leave! This gave him ample time to hitch bike home. Sometimes there were reports of possible raids by the IRA, and in the event of a raid they were ordered to lock themselves in a cell and let the terrorists take what they wanted!

The last six months of his service was spent at RAF Brampton, in Cambridgeshire, using his draughtsmanship skills to help produce training manuals. He also managed to do some flying. At RAF St Mawgan, an air-sea rescue station in Cornwall, where they presented a new colour to the station, he was taken up in a Sea King helicopter. As it had no doors, he felt somewhat anxious! He also had a very noisy flight in a Shackleton, a long range patrol aircraft of the type flown by Mike Mansley (q.v.), which was sometimes described as 'forty thousand rivets in close formation'!

Despite feeling that his National Service was largely a matter of filling in two years, and had not brought any real benefits in terms of personal development, he did not dislike the RAF and gave some thought to signing on, but decided in the end that it offered an uncertain future, and so returned to his civilian drawing board and decent wages.

Martin Patten

Royal Electrical and Mechanical Engineers 1955-57

Martin had the unique but dubious distinction of having been a mutineer during his National Service! He was based at Arborfield, near Reading, at the time. It was a period of high security following a raid on the armoury by the IRA and the theft of a number of weapons, resulting in many extra night time guard duties. There was much discontentment about this, and one day, pencilled in at the bottom of the day's duty list, were the words 'Hate Session. Lights Out.' Martin did not know what this meant, but that night, after he had gone to bed, he found out.

All was quiet, and then, gradually, he became aware of the word "Hate! Hate! Hate!" being chanted over and over from a nearby window. He and his room-mates ran to their window, opened it, and realised that the words were not coming just from one window, but from an ever-increasing number of them. "Hate! Hate! Hate!" was building up to a crescendo which reached every corner of the camp and well beyond. Martin and his mates joyfully added their voices to the hundreds of others in this spontaneous act of insubordination.

However, the Army does not tolerate insubordination, and inevitably, authority soon arrived in the form of the Company Sergeant Major and a marching squad of guards. How was he to deal with this mutiny? He could not arrest the entire camp, nor did he attempt to do so. Instead, he pointed at random to one man on the second floor and said "Arrest that man!" The chanting immediately stopped, and the only sound then to be heard was the clumping of heavy boots up the stairs to the victim's room. He was dragged downstairs and marched away to the guard house. Chastened, everyone went back to bed. The mutiny was over.

This was not the end of the matter, however. A week later, the entire company was summoned to the parade ground and lined up all around the sides. The arrested man was brought out to the middle of the square, and in full public view was charged with mutiny, stripped of his insignia and sentenced to detention at the Military Prison in Colchester, a place with a fearsome reputation for harsh discipline. The hapless man was never seen again.

It was, of course, grossly unfair to punish one man among the hundreds who had taken part in this act of insubordination, but the message it sent was clear: the Army does not tolerate mutiny, and if this happens again, it could be *you* who is arrested! Nor was punishment restricted to this one individual. Over the next few weeks, many found themselves doing 'jankers' (i.e. minor punishments) for the most trivial of offences.

Guard duties, the cause of the mutiny, continued at the rate of one or two a week. They ran from 6 pm to 6 am, during which two hours were spent on duty and four off, then another two on and another four off. During the 'off' periods they might be able to snatch some sleep in the noisy guard room, but there was no time off the next day to compensate for lost sleep. Small wonder the men became resentful as the cumulative tiredness of regular guard duties set in. Unlike the RAF, the Army did not give men time off the following day!

Martin had deferred his call-up until he had finished his degree in chemical engineering, so he was 21 when, on 24th November 1955, he boarded the train to Honiton, in Devon, where he had been told to report for his basic Army training. When it arrived at the station, almost all the passengers were young men carrying suitcases, all bound for the same destination - the training camp. A sergeant awaited them, and his first words left them in no doubt that they would from now on be doing everything in response to orders. "Come on, get fell in, get a move on!" he barked, and off they marched to the camp.

Then began a process of stripping away every shred of their civilian identity. The emphasis throughout this period was for the men to bond with each other, so that the safety and well-being of their mates became crucially important. In this way they were being prepared for battle situations, where every man looked out not only for himself but for his comrades.

During this initial period they were given tests to assess which regiments they would be assigned to, and Martin was selected to train as a radar mechanic. First, however, he went for a medical examination. At that point he expected, because of his education, to be selected for officer training. The conversation with the Medical Officer went something like this:

M.O.: You have a perforated eardrum

Martin: Yes. I had scarlet fever as a child, and this was the result.

M.O.: I recommend that you don't fire a gun.

Martin: All right, sir.

M.O.: Are you going to fire a gun?

Martin: No, sir. You've just told me not to.

M.O.: That's not the attitude we expect from our officers. You are obviously unsuitable.

On the strength of this interview, Martin was rejected for officer training. It was his introduction to the sometimes bizarre mentality of the Army. He never did fire a gun during his service.

Pay during basic training was one pound eight shillings a week (£1.40 in today's money). Though worth a lot more then, it was still abysmally meagre (average civilian wages were around £8 a week). Out of this they had to provide washing powder for their clothing (only their bedding was laundered), polish for their boots and brasses, hair cream, shaving soap, and razor blades. In the NAAFI (Navy, Army and Air Force Institute) they could purchase cigarettes, tobacco, coffee and other items to make life bearable. If they could afford it, they could go to the GAPH (Garrison Army Picture House).

When his basic training was over, Martin was posted to train as a radar mechanic at Arborfield, where the aforementioned mutiny took place. In November 1956, now with the rank of Craftsman (the equivalent of Private in other regiments) he was sent to the School of Anti-Aircraft Artillery at Manorbier, in Pembrokeshire, where his job was to maintain the radar systems that predicted where the enemy aircraft was going so that the gunners could shoot it down. They were, of course, firing at towed drogues rather than actual aircraft, and Martin was most unimpressed with the accuracy of their shooting. Hundreds of shells were fired for every target hit. Manorbier was a pleasant posting. The regime was relaxed, and they had exclusive use of the nearby beaches, which were closed to the public, and for Martin it was not too far to get home when he was on leave.

David Slaughter
RAF 1955-57

From insurance office clerk to air radar mechanic on V bombers was quite a career change for David, from Beckenham, Kent. Although the RAF was reluctant to train National Servicemen for this trade, regarding it as poor value for money given the time it took to train them and the limited length of their subsequent service, they found that the regulars (usually apprentices) were failing the tests whereas the National Servicemen were passing. So David was selected for radar training after completing his 'square bashing' at West Kirby, during which he had the unique experience of being part of the funeral cortege for Lord Trenchard, the founder of the RAF.

The cortege was made up of recruits from camps all around the country who were in their final week of training and whose marching was therefore of a high standard (unlike the rest of the RAF, which was, with notable exceptions, not generally renowned for its marching ability!). Preparation for this event involved a temporary move to RAF Uxbridge, which delayed the start of David's trade training. For this he was posted to RAF Yatesbury, Wilts. From here he managed to get home most weekends on the back of his friend Reg's motor bike.

Once qualified, he was posted to 543 Bomber Squadron at RAF Wyton, near Huntingdon, a photo reconnaissance station. Here he serviced the radar equipment on Valiants (one of the three V-bombers, the others being the Vulcan and the Victor). If he was on first line servicing he had to be available 24/7 as aircraft could arrive at any time of the day or night. His job was to trace any defective equipment, remove it and send it to the technical department to be opened up and repaired. This was called second line servicing and was carried out during normal daytime hours, and the mechanics alternated between the two. The disadvantage of being on first line was that in shared rooms sleep was often interrupted by the comings and goings of others. However, David overcame this by developing the ability to sleep through any amount of noise!

The workshops had to be scrupulously clean, as even a tiny particle of dust could affect the

Lord Trenchard, 'Father of the RAF'; statue on the Embankment, London .

equipment while fault finding and repairing went on. Outdoor clothing had to be left outside, and once a month each man had to spend an entire day with a vacuum cleaner removing all traces of dust and dirt. David took trade tests up to the level of Senior Aircraftman (SAC), which earned him the princely sum of eleven shillings and sixpence a day. He felt aggrieved at the time that National Insurance contributions were deducted, but when he retired many years later, he was grateful that these deductions ensured he would receive a full pension.

David took full advantage of the opportunities provided for sport, and played a lot of cricket and football as well as regularly swimming. He only recalls once having to go on parade, on Remembrance Day in Huntingdon. Towards the end of his service he was sent, for some reason, on a two-week firefighting course near Blackpool, and another fortnight's course at Moreton in Marsh, in the Cotswolds. Here they drove the famous Green Goddesses, later brought out of retirement for use by the Army when civilian firefighters went on strike.

During the Suez Crisis of 1956, all leave was cancelled. Cameras were removed from the Valiants and bomb racks were fitted. They then flew off to Aden, there to carry out bombing missions over Egypt. Fortunately, the operation was called off before this happened. But an unexpected consequence was that many men came back with dysentery. The drains overflowed and this caused an outbreak in the camp, which had to be sealed off, food being left at the gate. Unfortunately, David was one of the first victims, having collapsed at work. He was admitted to the sick bay, but such was the scale of the epidemic that beds soon ran out and billets had to be used as isolation units to accommodate the many victims. Fortunately, they all recovered.

David enjoyed his time in the RAF but was never tempted to stay on once his National Service was over.

Clive Mort

RAF 1951-53

For some men, National Service would change the whole future course of their lives. One such man was Clive Mort, from Briton Ferry, near Swansea, who, whilst serving in the RAF, met the girl who would eventually become his wife.

Boys who had been to boarding school were at a definite advantage when it came to National Service, for they had already endured and learned to cope with the painful experience of homesickness. At the tender age of eleven, Clive had become a boarder at Christ College in Brecon, and was therefore well equipped to deal with being plucked away from the comforts of home and family when he began his RAF service seven years later.

This was not the only advantage of his public school education.

Whilst at Brecon he had voluntarily joined the Combined Cadet Force, where he had gained such important skills for service life as competence at drilling a squad and the ability to assemble a Bren Gun. He had passed his Parts 1 and 2 Training Certificates, which, unbeknown to him at the time, would exempt him from two weeks of arduous 'square bashing'.

Clive began his National Service at RAF Padgate, Lancs, where, in his words, "a holiday camp atmosphere prevailed, which I have since concluded was purposefully arranged that way so that new entrants would report positively to their families in their first letters home." This 'honeymoon period' changed dramatically when he was then posted for eight weeks basic training at RAF Hednesford, Staffs "where my RAF experience was alarmingly different. The emphasis was on discipline, where orders were obeyed without question and no argument accepted," Consequently, his exemption from the final two weeks of this harsh regime left him feeling like a prisoner who has unexpectedly been given early release!

Clive was transferred to RAF Yatesbury, Wilts, where for the next twelve weeks he learned to become a radar operator. Then, to his great disappointment, he was posted to RAF West Beckham, in Norfolk, a very long way from his native Wales. But this was at the height of the Cold War, and Britain's defences were situated all along the east coast of England in anticipation of a possible attack by the Soviet Union. Radar scanners were the eyes that constantly searched for a potential enemies. It was far from glamorous work. Operators worked a 24 hour shift system, staring into their screens and identifying from blips the movement of aircraft in their sector of the North Sea and reporting through headsets to a Plotting Centre the co-ordinates, to allow aircraft to be monitored and tracked. If considered to be a threat, then standby aircraft could be scrambled to intercept the intruders, hopefully before any damage could be done.

Because of the distance involved, it was impossible for Clive to get home on a 48 hour pass. However, at Yatesbury he had become a close friend of a fellow airman called Barry Barnes, whose home was the village of Haslingfield, near Cambridge. Clive was invited to spend his short passes there, and it was on the first of these visits that he met Barry's sister, Avryl. An immediate mutual attraction blossomed with successive visits, and after leaving the RAF he was able to get a job in the Eastern Counties, which enabled him to continue seeing Avryl. Ultimately, they were married in Cambridge and had two children.

Despite having a suitable educational background, Clive was never offered a commission, but was satisfied to become a Senior Aircrafts-man. He played rugby and cricket for the station, and enjoyed the close comradeship of service life.

He wrote "In conclusion, I must say that while I would not have chosen to give up two years of my life to National Service, I made the best of it, and in the end saw it as an opportunity which I certainly turned to my advantage."

Alan Williams

RAF 1946-48

There must be very few airmen who can claim to have passed his rifle to an Air Vice Marshal to hold while he adjusted his belt, but Alan Williams was one of them. It was during a major inspection that Air Vice Marshal Brooke-Popham stopped in front of Aircraftman Williams, took one look at his rather sloppy belt and said "You want to do something about that belt!" He did not, of course, mean that the necessary adjustment be made there and then, but that was how Alan understood it. Needing both his hands free, he said "Hold this a minute", handed his rifle to the AVM and proceeded to tighten his belt so that it was no longer sloppy, then relieved the astonished officer of the weapon. One would have expected this act of apparent disrespect to have earned Alan at least a week of 'jankers', but amazingly no punishment ensued, and the incident became the subject of much subsequent amusement.

Alan, from Briton Ferry, near Swansea, was very annoyed that the war ended just before he was old enough to for military service. His brother had fought in North Africa and Italy, and Alan felt cheated of the chance to follow in his footsteps. Called up into the RAF in September 1946, he did three months basic training at West Kirby (where he actually enjoyed the drill) before being selected for training as a wireless/radar mechanic. He was sent to Keevil, in Wiltshire, to await allocation for training. Life was relatively pleasant there. He was free every weekend, could go home once a month and was able to hitch hike to London from time to time. (Hitch hiking, almost unknown today, was an easy way to travel at no cost. Drivers in those days were always willing to pick up a man in uniform.)

However, the worst winter of the century brought Alan's service to a sudden temporary halt. In February 1947, when the snow drifts were ten feet deep, he, together with most of the RAF personnel in Britain, was ordered to make his way home 'by any means possible', and having managed to complete this very difficult journey he spent the next ten weeks in the comfort of his home.

Recalled to Keevil in April, he spent some time testing radios in Hurricanes, the famous Battle of Britain fighters that were then still in service. He recalls a Jamaican flying instructor crash landing a Hurricane, which ended up at an angle of 45 degrees to the ground. The instructor emerged unhurt and slid down the wing, but then, to everyone's surprise, was seen to scramble back up and dive into the cockpit to retrieve his parachute, so as to avoid being on a charge for not wearing it! He was only just in time. Flames were starting to emerge from the engine, and within minutes the whole aircraft was ablaze!

Alan was then posted to Yatesbury for the first half of the wireless/ radar mechanic training course, which he completed, then transferred to Cranwell, the home of the RAF College, for the remaining four or five months of the course, but it was abruptly terminated within a few weeks. He was not told why, but assumed that it was too expensive and no longer cost effective, since his demob was only a few months away.

He was then reallocated to Spitalgate, where he was assigned to 'General Duties', i.e. whatever jobs needed doing. It was really a matter of filling in the last six months until demob. He was employed as a steward in the Sergeants' Mess, and on one occasion he was flown with others in a de Havilland Dominie to somewhere in Northamptonshire to clear up the base. Why they were flown this relatively short distance was a mystery, but it would have been better to have transported them by lorry, as they were all airsick, and some poor souls had the unpleasant task of cleaning out the aircraft afterwards!

Alan would like to have been a pilot, and certainly his A Levels in maths and physics would have qualified him, but he would have had to sign on for five years, and this he was not willing to do. He was demobbed in August 1948, and within a week was taken on as a trainee draughtsman with the Steel Company of Wales, so there was no problem of adjusting to civilian life.

He found the experience of National Service both enjoyable and beneficial from a life's experience point of view. It had given him the opportunity to travel to other parts of the UK and associate with boys of different nationalities and backgrounds. His grammar school years, from 12 to 18, were the war years 1940 to 1946, and until conscription he had not had any association with anyone other than his family and school friends.

RAF College Cranwell. Non-commissioned Airmen and Officers made history in October 2018 as they graduated together for the first time.

David Collins

Royal Corps of Signals 1960-62

Since the 1960s, homosexuality has not only become accepted but also celebrated. It was very different up till 1965, when it was a criminal offence. An incident which shows very clearly the difference in attitude to homosexuality in those days occurred one night when David was on guard duty. Having spotted a light in a room which should have been in darkness, he reported it to his sergeant major, who went with him to investigate. They discovered two men in bed together, and they were promptly arrested. They were sentenced to detention in the military prison at Colchester, commonly known as 'The Glasshouse' because the original building had a glass roof.

David, together with the sergeant major, had to escort the prisoners to this fearsome place, and he was appalled at what he saw. They were taken into a huge open space, like an aircraft hangar. Each man had a six foot by six foot floor space marked out by studs, in which was a mattress, a toilet and a wash basin. There was nothing to sit on, and no privacy whatsoever. No man was allowed to step over the studs marking out his space without permission. The prison was run by the Military Police (the so-called Redcaps), who ruled with an iron rod. Its purpose was to persuade serious offenders of the error of their ways, and few who served time there ever went back.

A typical activity would be to be taken to a room where a ton of coal stood at one end. The prisoner had to move the coal to the other end, clean and whitewash the area previously occupied by the coal, then move the coal back to the original end and repeat the whitewashing process. This operation would be endlessly repeated throughout the day. The regime at Colchester was brutal but effective in deterring its clients from making a repeat visit.

David was among the last batch of recruits to leave Cardiff General Station for National Service. A former pupil of Monkton House, a semi-military school in Cardiff, David was partly prepared for National Service when he was called up. He would like to have been a para-trooper (there was a Parachute Regiment Depot next to the school), but at six feet he was too tall. Instead, by way of total contrast, he became a trainer of teleprinter engineers. In the days when computers were in their infancy, a teleprinter was a vital piece of communication equipment, and the ability to repair a malfunctioning machine was an essential skill. Although he was promoted to corporal, this did not leave him financially any better off. Out of his fifteen shilling per week pay, ten was deducted to send to his disabled mother.

David had hoped to be posted overseas, having been assured by his older brother that he could be sent anywhere in the world. In fact, however, he was posted to the School of Signals at Catterick, in Yorkshire, and there he stayed for his entire service. One consolation, though, was that one of his close friends came from Bolton, in Lancashire, not far away, and they would travel at weekends on David's motor bike to his friend's home.

An amusing memory was being sent to Darlington to collect the garrison's wages, which for 15,000 personnel amounted to many thousands of pounds. One would have expected such a sum to have been protected by the highest level of security, but in fact David was issued with just a sub machine gun... and no bullets!

A more painful memory was the incident in the gym when, unsupervised by any PT instructor, he vaulted over a horse but missed and landed on his head, knocking himself unconscious. Fortunately, no damage was done and David completed his National Service without further mishap.

Mike Stubbs

RAF 1958-61

Mike's entry into the world of work was rather a rough one. Having left public school he went to work in his father's haulage business on a wage of thirteen shillings and ninepence a week! Mr Stubbs had formerly been the agent for Sir Lindsay Parkinson on the building of the Bridgend Arsenal in 1936-39.

Mike's pay would considerably increase when he signed on for an extra year of National Service in the RAF, as this entitled him to the princely sum of three pounds seventeen and six a week! He did his basic training at Wilmslow, where, amongst other things, he had his first lesson in race relations. One of his fellow trainees was black, and in those politically incorrect days it was not considered wrong to address a coloured man as 'Sambo', but this particular man strongly objected to the title. However, after a minor scuffle they became good friends.

After passing out Mike went to Netheravon to train for the RAF police, but a road accident while he was home on leave left him convalescing for six months and ended the possibility of continued service in the police. Having recovered, he re-mustered in Cardington and was posted as a storeman to Kirton Lindsay, Lincolnshire. This was quite a long way from home, but on one occasion he had the most amazing luck. Thumbing a lift, as most servicemen did in those days, from outside the camp, he told the driver he was going to South Wales.

"So am I" said the driver, "Whereabouts?"

"Porthcawl", said Mike.

"Well, that's where I'm going! To the Seabank Hotel. Where in Porthcawl do you live?"

"Just round the corner from the Seabank!"

So Mike had a lift literally from door to door. Few hitch hikers ever had such an easy ride!

Later he was posted to Innsworth, which was nearer to home, but then he discovered that he could do an exchange posting with someone from the Gloucestershire area who was currently at St Athan, just twenty miles from Porthcawl. So the exchange was made, and for eighteen months Mike lived at home and travelled each day on his scooter to St Athan, where he worked in the VOG (Victor on the Ground) section.

Mike described life at St Athan as 'a very cushy number'. He was paid to travel and to live out. The officer he worked for was a golf enthusiast, and was quite happy to leave Mike to cover while he went off to the golf course. Taking full advantage of this temporary authority, Mike, needing on one occasion to go to RAF Finningley, in Yorkshire, ordered up an Anson aircraft and was flown there!

Not surprisingly, Mike very much enjoyed his National Service. Though interrupted by the period of convalescence, he was able latterly to enjoy living at home and being paid to do so, and at the same time being given a great deal of freedom in his work.

Signing On

A s they came to the end of their two years, many National Servicemen were invited to sign on for a longer period, especially when
National Service was coming to an end and the high command was
anxious to maintain an adequate level of manpower afterwards. Most
declined the invitation, but two of my interviewees, Bill Lee and David
Geary-Andrews, did sign on and made the RAF their career.

Bill Lee

RAF 1957-91

When Bill began his National Service in the RAF in 1957, he had
absolutely no idea that two years would eventually extend to thirty four
and that he would rise through the ranks to retire as a Squadron Leader,
having collected the awards of BEM and MBE on the way!

Bill deferred his National Service till he was 21 in order to complete
his apprenticeship as a joiner at the Carriage and Wagon Works in
Derby. He continued to work as a joiner in the RAF, and was persuaded
to sign on for an extra year, which would give him automatic promotion
to Senior Aircraftman (SAC), but further promotion unexpectedly came
when he was posted to RAF Upwood. It happened that most of the
technicians were about to be demobbed, and Bill was promoted to
Acting Corporal in charge of the workshop. From there he went to RAF
Weeton, where he actually got to work on aircraft.

In November 1958 he was posted to Nicosia, in Cyprus, where he
worked on the Bristol 181 helicopter, which had wooden blades. He

was there for two and a half years and was now a Corporal Technician.

By the time his three years National Service was over Bill decided to sign on for nine years. He was posted to the RAF College at Henlow, where he had the interesting job of making models of Russian missiles, based on covertly obtained photographs. These would be tested in wind tunnels to assess their capabilities. He was now a Senior Technician (equal to Sergeant), so was steadily working his way up the ranks.

His next posting was to RAF Bruggen, in Germany. On returning to the UK he went to RAF St Athan, in South Wales, where his job was bullet-proofing Land Rovers for service in Northern Ireland. For this work he was awarded the British Empire Medal and promoted to Flight Sergeant. The normal next step would have been Warrant Officer, the highest non-commissioned rank, but instead he was offered a commission, and with the rank of Flying Officer he became Motor Transport (MT) Officer at RAF High Wycombe.

Possibly Bill's most interesting job was as Technical Director for the Royal Tournament. As an officer with woodwork experience he was ideally qualified. For this work he was awarded the MBE.

His final promotion was to Squadron Leader at RAF Brize Norton, where he was in charge of the mechanical engineering squadron. His last tour was at RAF St Athan, Glamorgan, and he retired from the RAF on his 55th birthday.

Bill's story is an example of the way National Service could take a man in a totally unexpected direction in his life. When he was called up he intended only to do his two years then resume his career as a joiner on the railways. Yet as one opportunity after another came his way, he was sufficiently flexible to see the benefits of pursuing an altogether different career path which led him to success and acclaim beyond anything he could ever have imagined!

David 'Andy' Geary-Andrews

RAF 1955-85

Another man for whom National Service led to a lifetime career, Andy, as he prefers to be known, joined the RAF after completing his apprenticeship as a carpenter and joiner. He trained as an airframe fitter at No 4 School of Technical Training, RAF St Athan, in South Wales, and was then posted to Feltwell, Norfolk, where he was put to work servicing the Provost, the RAF's main initial training aircraft at the time. In his own words "It would have been difficult to find a simpler aircraft to work on" He very much enjoyed "having aeroplanes to play with all day", and when his National Service came to an end he signed on for five years and then kept extending it until he had finally clocked up 30 years!

From Feltwell he was posted to Cranwell, the home of the RAF College, where he worked on Vampires. In contrast to the Provost, these were, "Horrible aircraft – the designers had given no thought to servicing". Then came an overseas posting, to RAF Seletar, in Singapore. He sailed out on the Oxfordshire, the last troopship to be used to transport personnel to overseas bases before being replaced by aircraft. Seletar was a busy station, where you never knew what aircraft were arriving next - Dakotas, Shackletons, Chipmunks, Vampires, Belvedere and Whirlwind helicopters, each presenting a new challenge to the maintenance crews.

He thought Singapore a lovely city, where all three races (Indian, Chinese and Malay) lived harmoniously together. He recalls a trip to the uninhabited island of Ubin, where they spend a wonderful day walking through virgin jungle. Life was easy at Seletar. They had an 'amah', or servant, to clean their billet and polish their shoes. He was known as 'Pop', a lovely man, everyone's idea of a grandad!

After two and a half years Andy was posted back to the UK, to 390 MU (Maintenance Unit) at Bicester, from where they were sent all over the country to other stations to do jobs that were beyond the ability of their own technicians. Then to RAF Lyneham, Wiltshire, where he met his wife, a WAAF driver, after which came another overseas posting, this time for a thirteen-month tour at RAF Muharraq in the Persian Gulf.

The BAC Jet Provost, in use with the RAF from 1955 to 1993

This was not the particularly welcome, as he had to go two weeks before their first wedding anniversary and return two weeks after their second! Such was life in the forces. Here they serviced and refuelled VC10s. He said sarcastically that Muhurraq was a "wonderful beach...desert from one side to the other!"

From there he was posted to RAF Lynton on Ouse, where he worked on Jet Provosts, and then on to RAF Brawdy, servicing Hunters, "a nice plane to work on". He was there for about eight years. His final years were spent teaching apprentices at RAF St Athan, where he had trained all those years earlier.

As with Bill Lee, National Service had taken Andy's life in a totally unexpected direction. He said "I would never have gone into the RAF had it not been for National Service. I would have spent my life as a carpenter and joiner. What a different life that would have been!"

The Royal Navy

John Lewis

RN 1952-54

The Royal Navy was very reluctant to accept National Servicemen, believing that two years was not long enough to equip a man with the required skills. Consequently, only about five percent found themselves in the Senior Service, and one of them was John Lewis from Cardigan. What may perhaps have tipped the scales in his favour was the fact that he had completed a five year apprenticeship at the Royal Aircraft Establishment in Aberporth, West Wales, and had worked on guided missiles. Whatever the reason, he was taken on by the Navy, and after

a tough six weeks basic training at Victoria Barracks in Portsmouth, he was posted to the gunnery school at Whale Island where he qualified as a Petty Officer in charge of armament.

John was then posted to Malta, where he joined HMS Wrangler, an anti-submarine frigate. He soon got used to sleeping in a hammock, and was never troubled by seasickness despite experiencing some rough waters. The rest of his National Service can best be described as a

Mediterranean cruise! The ship paid courtesy visits to Greece, Spain, Gibraltar, Sicily and various North African ports. They did do some serious work, however, firing four inch shells at targets, though he confesses that they missed more than they hit! The only time he came anywhere near danger was in Egypt, when he had to take six men in a jeep from Suez to Port Said. This was a 'showing the flag' exercise, as at this time Egypt was still under British rule, but experiencing increasing resentment at the military presence, and the danger of this trip lay in the fact that British servicemen were likely to be fired on by terrorists. Fortunately, they were not, and returned unharmed.

While in Malta, John met some of the Royal Family, such as Prince Philip, who, as a Naval lieutenant, had been leading a very pleasant life there with his young wife until the death of King George VI meant that she became Queen and his promising career came to a premature end. He also met Lord Louis Mountbatten, the Queen's uncle, whom John describes as "...a real gentleman. He put you completely at your ease when he spoke to you."

A most unpleasant task on one occasion was searching for an airliner that had crashed into the sea. Using an anti-submarine detection unit with downward-facing cameras, they managed to locate the wreck, but did not find any bodies, although they did see items of baggage floating on the surface, which was very distressing.

One naval tradition that was still being observed (though these days no longer) was the daily issue of rum. Every morning at 11am "Up Spirits" would be called and the crew would line up for their ration. As a Petty Officer John had his rum neat, but ratings took it 'two on one', i.e. two parts water to one part rum. No doubt anything stronger might have impaired their efficiency on a fighting ship, but Petty Officers like John were evidently assumed to have stronger heads.

As a 21-year-old Petty Officer, and a National Serviceman to boot, John very occasionally encountered resentment from regulars who had taken years to reach this rank, but most accepted that he was entitled to this rank on account of his qualifications and knowledge of weapons.

John recalls with amusement the occasion when, on entering harbour in Malta, the stern of the ship hit the wall and was badly damaged. The captain, whose name was Parry, was known thereafter as 'Captain Crunch'!

John thoroughly enjoyed his National Service and was tempted to stay on, but his fiancee was not keen on the idea of becoming a naval wife, so he left at the end of his two years and became an engineer at the Steel Company of Wales.

Dennis Purchase

RN 1951-53

Another of the very few men who were accepted for National Service by the Navy was Dennis Purchase, from Porthcawl. He had put himself in a strong position for selection by serving first in the Sea Cadets and then the Royal Naval Volunteer Reserve, but nevertheless he very nearly ended up in the Army! He had deferred his call-up until he had completed his apprenticeship, but whilst doing his RNVR training at Portland, he was dismayed to receive a letter ordering him to report for Army training. However, it had come too late, as he had by then been accepted by the Navy. He had cause to be thankful, for had he gone into the Army he may well have been sent to fight in Korea, the very worst of the conflicts in which National Servicemen fought.

First, however, he had to endure six weeks of rigorous training at Victoria Barracks in Portsmouth, where he arrived on bitterly cold day in February 1951. Reporting as instructed at 1600 hours, he was dismayed to be told that everyone had gone home! They were not pleased to have to be recalled to process his arrival. After being given a mattress cover he was surprised to be sent to what appeared to be a stable. There he was told to fill it with straw! This was to be his mattress while he was there. The enormous dormitory which he shared with 39 others was almost impossible to heat. It had one large stove, and just one bucketful of coal to last all evening. Consequently it was never lit before 7 pm. They were not allowed out of camp for the entire six weeks, and had to spend their free time in a dismal NAAFI. However, unlike

Dennis Purchase, front row, second from left, with a group of trainee Petty Officers

some of his fellow recruits who had come straight from home into this harsh environment, Dennis's had been to some extent prepared for Navy life by his RNVR training.

As a qualified joiner, Dennis was automatically promoted to the rank of Acting Petty Officer, and his next posting was to the Petty Officer Training School at Corsham, near Bath, a far more comfortable billet, although the training was tough. They were set group tasks, such as hauling a full tank of water over various obstacles, success being measured by the amount of water remaining in the tank at the end.

They were dropped off from lorries in the middle of the countryside and, without the aid of maps, told to make their way back to camp. They had to pretend to be escaping prisoners, always on the lookout for other trainees who were trying to catch them. At one point Dennis hid in a chicken coop, and lay there listening to the sound of the running feet of his pursuers, expecting any second to be caught. But he was not found, and he made his way to a pub, where he asked where the nearest bus stop was. "Right across the road," said the barman, "and the bus will take you all the way back to camp." It was certainly his lucky day!

After further training in the workshops, Dennis was then sent back to Portsmouth to join HMS Maidstone, a large submarine depot ship with a crew of 1200, which rose to 1800 with the submarine crews, who slept on board. She was really a seagoing multi-purpose workshop, equipped with a foundry, shops for 29 painters, plumbers and joiners, machine shops, torpedo repair shops and plants for charging submarines' batteries. She was designed to look after nine operational submarines, and was able to carry out major repairs at sea if necessary. There were laundries, a cinema, hospital, chapel, two canteens, bakery and a fully equipped operating theatre and dental surgery.

It was in this large, self-sufficient floating community that Dennis spent the rest of his National Service. His work involved all aspects of joinery: making doors, cupboards, lockers, or repairing damage. For some of the time they were docked in Portsmouth, but when they went to sea his pay was increased by one and sixpence (7.5p in today's money) a day on top of the princely two pounds fourteen and sixpence (£2.75) a fortnight regular pay! Their journeys took them to the Shetlands, to Norway (where their uniforms caused some hostile looks, being similar to those of the German 'Kriegsmarine', or Navy). They also went to

HMS Maidstone, in service 1941-78. Submarine depot ship until 1969 she was refitted as accommodation for 2,000 troops in Belfast. In 1971, she was used as a prison ship in Operation Demetrius as a place to hold internees. (IWM).

Malta and Gibraltar, and on one occasion put in to the Spanish port of Corunna so that one of the crew could receive medical treatment that was beyond the facilities of the ship's own hospital. He was so well treated that when they came back for him three months later he was most reluctant to leave, no doubt because of the attention he had received from the Spanish nurses! This was the first time since the Civil War of 1936-39 that a British ship had entered a Spanish port.

As with John Lewis (q.v.), Dennis's promotion to Petty Officer caused grumbling from some of the 'old hands' who had taken fifteen years or more to reach this rank, and resented National Servicemen who were, in their words, 'barely there more than a dog watch' enjoying their hard-earned and cherished status and privileges! However, despite this Dennis enjoyed life, including his daily ration of rum, taken neat and not watered down 'two-on-one' like the lower ratings. Rum was used as a kind of currency; payment for favours done could be in a rum ration rather than in money. The extra allowance would be carefully bottled and saved for weekends on board when they could not go ashore. Another privilege of the PO's mess was the use of messmen, who, for a small fee, would fetch food up to their mess, thus avoiding the need to queue in a crowded galley.

One thing the navy did not tolerate was lateness, even when it was unavoidable. On one occasion Dennis's train was held up, which delayed his arrival back from leave. Nothing was said at the time, but when Maidstone arrived in Gibraltar a few weeks later and Dennis was eagerly preparing to go ashore, his was dismayed to learn that his earlier late return from leave meant he was on 'defaulters' and therefore confined to the ship while all his mates waved him goodbye from the liberty boat!

Unlike many National Servicemen, Dennis did not tick off the days till demob, and it was with some surprise that he learned he was due for release. His final days were spent idly hanging around the work-shops, unable to start any jobs because he would not be there to finish them. He felt depressed at having to leave the mates he had happily served with, and took a little time to adjust to civilian life. He was not finished with the Navy, however, for he was required to spend five years in the RNVR, and this involved being called up for two weeks' service each year, which he enjoyed.

Keith Williams

RN 1955-57

A list of the places visited by Keith's ship reads like the itinerary of a present day luxury cruise: Bermuda, Miami, Nassau, Caracas, Rio, Jamaica, Grenada, Trinidad, Venezuela, Pensacola, New Orleans, Port of Spain, Tristan da Cuhna, Cape Town, Mombasa. These were all ports at which his ship, HMS Kenya, a light cruiser with a complement of 750, paid 'showing the flag' visits, warmly welcomed wherever it went. He was on Kenya from October 1955 until November 1956.

However, naval life was not all fun and games. There was important work to be done, such as ferrying Royal Marines up the Red Sea to Aden to protect the oilfields when the 'Seven Day War' broke out, and bringing them back when it was over. The ship spent a total of thirteen weeks in Aden during the crisis, until finally departing for Durban for refuelling and returning to the UK in November 1956.

There was a most unpleasant incident during a firework display for the benefit of the local people when a bank of several rockets blew up and three men were badly burned. Unfortunately, one died on the way to the hospital. Keith received a commendation for his prompt action in getting the fire main pumps to full pressure and putting the fire out, though he modestly claimed he was only doing his job.

The few who were accepted by the Navy for National Service either had a special skill or, as with Keith, a relative who had served at sea, in his case his uncle, a wartime seaman. Prior to joining the Navy, Keith had been a railway fireman, but although he was classified as a stoker on the ship, that role no longer involved shovelling coal. The ship was oil burning, so his job was to operate the boilers while at sea and to undertake work in the engine room when they were docked. He was really a mechanical engineer rather than a stoker, but the Navy liked to hang on to its traditional titles. One of his additional jobs while in port was testing the water drawn from the sea for drinking purposes to make sure it was fully desalinated and for filling up the boilers as no salt water was allowed to contaminate the boilers when in use.

As was normal practice at sea, the men worked four hours on and four hours off. In his free time Keith entertained his messmates with his piano playing, sometimes duetting, or watched films in the cinema on board. When they went ashore they enjoyed the hospitality of local people, such as when he and his mate were invited home for tea by two girls who worked in the Woolworths Store in Miami. However, in Cape Town he became very aware of Apartheid. They were told not to talk to black people and to keep to white areas. Keith found this very hard to accept, especially as they had just come from Jamaica, where racial segregation did not exist.

Keith found sleeping in hammocks very comfortable, because he never felt the movement of the ship. He was only troubled by seasickness on one occasion when the waves were particularly high. It lasted for about three days and never returned.

Although he very much enjoyed his time in the Navy, Keith did not sign on for five years, wishing to return to his home and family, which he had seen very little of during the two years. It had been like a very pleasant extended cruise, but in the end he wanted to get back to real life.

Non-Combatant Service

Dennis Tomlin

Conscientious Objector 1949-51

Although National Service was compulsory, allowance was made for those who, for reasons of conscience, did not wish to serve in the armed forces. As an alternative, they were required to do some kind of community work for two years. Exemption was normally granted on religious grounds, but applicants had to face a tribunal whose job it was to assess their sincerity. One of those who chose this option was Dennis Tomlin.

Dennis was born in 1930 in Gillingham, Kent, the son of a Royal Marine Sergeant Physical Training Instructor. When the war broke out, Dennis and his sister Doreen were evacuated to Aberkenfig for eighteen months, then moved to Burgess Hill in 1941. He attended Lewes County Grammar School, and it was during these years that he began to question "the Anglican Church's support of the war and its integration into the English establishment". When his parents divorced in 1946, he and Doreen stayed with their mother.

Having obtained his School Certificate he enrolled on an Architectural Studies course at Brighton College of Art. There he joined a Quaker Centre, and discovered that the movement offered an alternative to compulsory military service. On his college course he talked to men and women who had served in the armed forces and found them supportive of his objections, saying that they had fought the war to preserve freedom of conscience. In 1949, knowing that he would eventually be called up, he left his studies after the intermediate exam and enrolled in a Quaker alternative service for young objectors.

He was duly called before a tribunal in Putney. There he was questioned by the three people, a lawyer, a clergyman and a trade union official, sitting up on a raised judge's bench. He found it gruelling, but he was granted exemption to serve with the Quaker FAU (Friends' Ambulance Unit) International Service.

For the next two years he would be doing manual and agricultural work, and the first three months were spent training at the FAU headquarters near Petersfield, Hampshire. "It was hard work, getting up early for a three mile run, then threshing corn or digging drains... After the blisters healed, our hands were hardened, our muscles strengthened for the future pick and shovel peace work that we were to do." Then they worked in farming, forestry and hospitals to earn money to support teams in Europe, which was beginning to recover from the ravages of war. Dennis was posted to forestry units in Cumberland and on the Scottish border, but was then unexpectedly sent to France to replace a volunteer who had been repatriated because his mother was ill. Dennis was chosen because he could speak French.

His first posting was to work with other Conscientious Objectors (COs) and international volunteers to establish a village for war orphans at Vercheny, in the lower Alps. A group of young adults had taken over some neglected vineyards and deserted houses and had brought sixty children from Paris to live there. "It was chaotic but exciting, challenging but also rewarding. We worked to rehabilitate some village houses and build new ones, to build a new school and bring a new water pipeline from a source high up in the mountains... to supplement the only existing supply in the fountain in the village square." At Christmas, by which time the deep winter snow made outdoor work impossible, the group members were repatriated.

Dennis's second posting was to Tannay, in central France, where with another CO he helped to convert an ancient convent into a workers' holiday home. "Although it was hard work, it was a rich experience, living in a small country town in deepest France, fraternising with the young people there but also meeting workers from Paris who came at weekends to help with the painting and decorating."

It was to a Quaker community farm at Champcevrais, in the Yonne, that Dennis went for his third posting. Here he joined a small group of four COs doing a variety of agricultural work: clearing overgrown hedges, sawing wood for fuel, picking the apples and preparing them to be turned into 'Eau de Vie de Pomme'. He remained friends with the Schultz family, who ran the farm, for the rest of his life.

Then it was back to England and work in a forestry gang in Sussex until his service with the FAU ended in the spring of 1951 after two years and sixty days.

Dennis's work with the FAU had enabled him to fulfil his obligation to do National Service in a way that did not require him to take human life. It had also given him the benefit of healthy outdoor work as well as the chance to immerse himself in French life and language. But there was a further benefit: during his time in France he met the woman who would eventually become his wife.

However, the course of true love did not run as smoothly as he would have liked, at least not at first. He met Francoise at Vercheny early in 1950, but later that year she returned to Algiers to resume her studies. A month later, Dennis obtained ten days' leave to hitch hike to Algiers to ask her to marry him when they were both free, but, sadly, this was not the right time for her and he returned disappointed. However, to his surprise, she later arrived unexpectedly in Tannay to see him, and his hopes were revived, but he was careful not to mention marriage. She returned to Paris, leaving him disappointed again, but the following year, when he was working in Sussex, he received a postcard to say she was in London and would like to see him. They met in Westminster and had a wonderful day enjoying the sights of the Festival of Britain. "By the end of the day we knew we were a couple for life." They married in September 1952, and now live at Congenies, near Nimes.

Conscientious Objectors were not without their critics, even in peacetime. There were those who called them cowards for not being prepared to defend their country. Others, however, admired them for having the courage to face public hostility by refusing to do what went against their principles. They firmly believed that taking life was wrong, no matter what the cause. Just as if they had served in the armed forces, they had sacrificed two years of their lives, but could look back afterwards with a clear conscience and feel that they had made a difference to the communities they had served. So far from being cowards, they were men of courage.

I am most grateful to Mrs Doreen Lewis, Dennis's sister, who contacted him in France and asked him to provide me with an account of his National Service, from which I have quoted in this piece.

Epilogue

"They should bring back National Service!" was an oft-heard lament in the years following its abolition, a cry from the heart of the perplexed older generation when viewing a vandalised telephone box or a graffiti'd wall, convinced that a strong dose of military discipline would straighten out these mindless juvenile vandals.

This, of course, was to misunderstand the purpose of National Service. It was never intended to be a reform school for wayward youths, but a means of meeting Britain's postwar military commitments. The beneficial effects – pride in appearance, respect for authority, increased self confidence – were an unintended consequence.

It must be remembered that the young men who went through National Service had been brought up at a time when the ethos of the nation was service and duty in the common cause of winning the war. The generation born after 1945, the so-called 'baby boomers', grew up with a very different attitude. They had no memories of the war, and found tedious their parents' frequent references to its hardships. Unlike their older siblings, they did not aspire to emulate their elders; instead they espoused their own fashions and their own music, and along with that went a radically different attitude to society. Rather than conforming, they rebelled. For them it was no longer a matter of sacrificing the needs of the individual to the common cause; rather their aim was the achievement of personal satisfaction through enjoyment. "Do your own thing" replaced "Do your duty". It was probably as well that National Service ended in 1960. The conscripts of the next decade would undoubtedly have proved less malleable than their predecessors.

Those who called for the return of National Service overlooked one very obvious fact: their young men could be killed, not in the defence of their country but to prop up a disintegrating Empire. It was one thing to die in defence of loved ones against a barbaric enemy; it was quite another to sacrifice one's life in a faraway country, fighting against people who only demanded the freedom to run their own affairs. Altogether, 395 National Servicemen were killed in action.

National Service was expensive. Keeping thousands of young men out of the workforce, feeding, clothing, housing and caring for them was a massive drain on the economy. By the late 1950s Britain no longer faced the huge defence commitments of 1945. Many former colonies had now achieved independence, or were soon to do so, and the Suez fiasco had shattered the illusion that Britain was still a great power. The nuclear deterrent had rendered unnecessary a large army to repel an invasion; the only need for conventional troops was now as part of our NATO commitment in Germany, and to deal with local outbreaks of trouble in the Commonwealth. There was a growing clamour to end National Service.

However, it was not only increased public disapproval that brought it to an end; the service chiefs themselves no longer saw the need for large numbers of reluctant conscripts to fill the ranks. They now wanted willing volunteers who saw military service as a career, not a chore.

National Service was abolished on 31st December 1960, and the last National Serviceman to be demobilised was 2nd Lieutenant Richard Vaughan on 16th May 1963.

About the Author

Malcolm Cowper was born in 1946 in Bridgwater, Somerset, and the following year moved with his family to South Wales, where he was educated at Bridgend Boys' Grammar School. After teacher training at Sheffield University he taught secondary English in Rotherham and Chesterfield, retiring in 1997 as a Deputy Head.

He was 14 when National Service ended, and has heard mixed views about it throughout his life, ranging from "I wouldn't have missed it for the world" to "Two utterly wasted years"! He decided to find out more, and talked to some 60 former National Servicemen. This book is the result of these fascinating conversations.

Malcolm now lives back in South Wales, in the seaside town of Porthcawl, where he is surrounded by a large and loving family. He enjoys walking, writing, choral singing, watching rugby and learning Welsh. He has published two books of wartime memories: *Derbyshire's Unsung Heroes* (2013) and *Glamorgan's Greatest Generation* (2016).